People, Places, and Books

ALSO BY GILBERT HIGHET:

The Classical Tradition: Greek and Roman Influences on Western Literature (Oxford University Press, 1949)

The Art of Teaching (Knopf, 1950)

FORTHCOMING:

Juvenal the Satirist (Oxford University Press, 1953)

People
Places
and
Books

Gilbert Highet

New York / OXFORD UNIVERSITY PRESS / 1953

COPYRIGHT 1953 BY GILBERT HIGHET

Library of Congress Catalogue Card Number: 53-5549

'The Old Gentleman' copyright 1952 by Gilbert Highet

Third Printing, 1953

PRINTED IN THE UNITED STATES OF AMERICA

Preface

AT THE BEGINNING OF 1952, the President of the Oxford University Press in New York invited me to talk about literature once a week, over a local radio station. He did not ask me to recommend any publications of the Oxford Press, but left me perfectly free to speak about any book issued by any publisher in the United States or in Great Britain. The only stipulation he made was that the works discussed should either be books of a high standard or else open up some question of broad literary or social interest.

This volume contains thirty of the talks which I gave under that agreement, during 1952. They appear as they were first written, without the cuts which the exact timing of radio always makes necessary. Some deal with single authors, such as Dickens or Eliot. Some evoke regions described in literature—for instance, Byzantium. Some are about groups of works which belong together by plan, like the *Great Books,* or by convergence, like the books on imprisonment. I have added to each piece a list of the chief works mentioned in it, with the dates of publication and the publishers' names.

Let me thank my wife, who listened to all these talks before they were airborne, and made invaluable suggestions for their improvement. The novels about resistance to tyranny which she herself has published, under her pen-name of Helen MacInnes, would surely have been discussed in these pages were it not that the etiquette of criticism made such discussion impossible.

For their technical advice, their patience, and their good humor (recording and broadcasting are trickier than one might think), I should like to thank Mr. Fon Boardman of the Oxford University Press in New York, Mr. Andrew Stewart of Denhard and Stewart, the 'onlie begetter' of the entire series, and the expert of Nola Studios, Mr. Stanley Bumbly, who painlessly inserts a dropped *the* and extracts, noiselessly, a superfluous *but.*

Finally, let me thank the many listeners who have been kind enough to write me about these talks; and let me say that I hope they will enjoy them once again, in this slightly less ephemeral form.

G. H.

New York
February 1953

Acknowledgments

I SHOULD LIKE to express my thanks to a number of persons and firms who have been kind enough to grant me permission to reprint illustrative passages from works in which they hold copyright:

The Encyclopaedia Britannica, from Volume 1 of *Great Books of the Western World*;

Farrar, Straus & Young, Inc., from Edmund Wilson's *Classics and Commercials* (copyright 1950 by Edmund Wilson);

Harcourt, Brace and Company, Inc., from *Collected Poems 1909-1935* by T. S. Eliot (copyright 1936 by Harcourt, Brace and Company);

Alfred A. Knopf. Inc., from *The Later D. H. Lawrence,* edited by W. Y. Tindall;

Little, Brown & Company, from Frank Eaton's *Pistol Pete: Veteran of the Old West*;

The Macmillan Company, from W. B. Yeats' *The Tower*;

Random House, Inc., from Robinson Jeffers' *Roan Stallion* (copyright 1925 by Boni & Liveright, Inc.);

Charles Scribner's Sons, from Rolfe Humphries' translation of Vergil's
Aeneid;
The University of Chicago Press, from Richmond Lattimore's transla-
tion of Homer's *Iliad*;
The Viking Press, Inc., from Rebecca West's *Black Lamb and Grey
Falcon*;
Edmund Wilson, Esq., from his own poem, 'The Mass in the Parking
Lot,' published in *Wilson's Reliques of Ancient Western Poetry*;

and to any others who may inadvertently have been over-
looked.

Contents

PEOPLE

PLACES

BOOKS

People

Henry Fowler: Modern English Usage

READING books is a pleasure. But if it is a pleasure to read books, it is also a pleasure to talk about them. I suppose it is a way of reliving the pleasure the book gave us originally, when we first ate it and digested it. Gourmets, like Brillat-Savarin, do the same with meals which have been cooked and served to them long ago. The difference is that the gourmet has a diminishing pleasure, as time wears on. People who talk about books have a perpetual pleasure, and often an increasing pleasure as their taste grows finer, their memory richer.

There are not too many books which give us such pleasure. When we meet them, we recommend them to one another. One of my perennial favorites is *Modern English Usage,* by Henry Fowler, published in 1926, and still a heavy seller. I bought it first in 1929, when I went up to Oxford, and I am now on my second copy. It was, I believe, a standby of the late Alexander Woollcott; Harold Ross of *The New Yorker* was devoted to it; and one of the most battered copies I have ever seen was on the desk of the editor of a famous newspaper —he told me he used it every day, and sometimes every hour.

Before we look at this remarkable book, who was its author, Fowler himself? He was a strange fellow. He was one of those eccentrics who seem to be a special product of England—not the wild surrealist eccentrics, but the logical eccentrics, who decide exactly what to do in a large number of situations, do it with relentless consistency, and omit to notice that logical behavior often looks perfectly crazy to the rest of the world. He was rather like the White Knight in *Alice,* except that the Knight was ineffective while Fowler was ferociously efficient. If you had seen a little man with bright red cheeks, a great pointed beard, and a perfectly bald head, running briskly through the streets of London to bathe in the Serpentine (at least once breaking the ice to do so); or if you had seen him working at his proofs while sitting outside his cottage in the Channel Islands in a November sea-mist, wearing football shorts and a jersey (or should it be a guernsey?), you would have recognized one of the long line of English eccentrics which begins with Chaucer and is still flourishing in the person of Mr. Churchill.

Fowler was nearly seventy when the book came out: for he was born almost a century ago now, in 1858. He went to one of the private schools which the English persist in calling public schools (it was Rugby), and then on to Oxford, where he was at Balliol College and had a mediocre record. He spent the first seventeen years of his working life as a schoolmaster at Sedbergh; and he was apparently rather bad: the reverse of Mr. Chips. The boys called him 'Joey Stinker' because he smoked heavily. He had no distinguished pupils; he was too shy to teach well; all this period of his life was a failure which prepared him for his later success.

He gave up teaching at the age of forty-one, and went back to London to try free-lancing—for, like so many of the Englishmen we hear of in the nineteenth century, he had a private income: not much, but he was passing rich on £120 a year. After some time, the Oxford University Press learned of his undoubted talents and his wide knowledge of literature; and he was engaged to work upon the great *Oxford English Dictionary,* which thereafter became the focus of his life. (This makes him a fairly direct descendant of that other eccentric, Dr. Samuel Johnson.) In 1911, he brought out, as a by-product, a pocket dictionary which was not, like the big one, historically arranged, but straightforward and contemporary: *The Concise Oxford Dictionary of Current English.*

In the First World War he volunteered for ordinary service, at the age of fifty-seven (I *said* he was eccentric). He disguised his age as the acceptable one of forty-four. And, characteristically, he protested violently when he was not sent into the combat zone but kept unloading and guarding stores at a rear-area seaport. Finally he fell ill and was invalided out; his beloved brother Francis, who had worked with him and joined up with him, died of TB contracted in service. *Modern English Usage* was planned by the two, writing together, and is dedicated by Fowler to the memory of his brother.

He returned to civilian life and went on working on the *Oxford Dictionary,* writing a number of articles for specialist periodicals about the proper use of language, the avoidance of pedantry, and other subjects dear to his heart and his sharp, uncompromising, commonsensical mind. As the result of all the second twenty years of his career, *Modern English Usage* came out in 1926, was well received, and has been selling well ever since. He was astounded at the fan-mail which he got from all over the world, arguing, agreeing, contradicting, suggesting, admiring, or simply begging. A convict in a prison in California wrote and asked him for a free copy 'to prepare him for a literary career when he had served his time.' The man Fowler died in 1933, but the book—and this is the chief reason why people try to write good books—has gone on living.

And now, what about the book itself? *Modern English Usage* is set out like a dictionary; and indeed its full title is *A Dictionary of Modern English Usage*. But it gives much less information than a dictionary: hardly any derivations, no explanations of easy words, no attempt at completeness. In fact, it is a book about difficult and disputable words, habits, and groupings of words. Most of the information is given in short paragraphs. Let us look up one, and see how it works. What does *garble* mean? I am never quite sure myself. I should say a garbled story was a confused and unintelligible story, wouldn't you? Fowler will know, and he will tell us. Here he is:

> **garble.** The original meaning is to sift, to sort into sizes with a view to using the best or rejecting the worst. The modern transferred sense is to subject a set of facts, evidence, a report, a speech, &c., to such a process of sifting as results in presenting all of it that supports the impression one wishes to give of it & deliberately omitting all that makes against or qualifies this. **Garbling** stops short of falsification and misquotation, but not of misrepresentation; a garbled account is partial in both senses.

That is not quite typical of Fowler's style. His sentences are usually shorter, and more cutting. But it does give a fine impression of his clear, logical mind, and of his talent for conveying the maximum information without pedantry or waste of energy.

The paragraph also shows pretty clearly what the uses of the book are. Fowler had two chief aims in view. One was to help people who were vague or confused about the true meanings of words and the neatest and most exact methods of expression. Ought we to avoid a split infinitive at all costs? Is it necessary to say something like this: 'The four powers have combined to forbid flatly hostilities'—because we are afraid of saying 'to flatly forbid hostilities'? Fowler will argue it out, and make it clear to us.* The other purpose of his book was to prevent the corruption of our language by the intrusion of clumsy, careless, slipshod, or ignorant words and phrases. In speaking and writing, as in other things, we acquire bad habits very easily, and soon become unaware of them. They spread from one man to another, then from one generation to another; they can infect a whole epoch, and ruin what might have been forceful speech and convincing books. The only way to avoid such habits is constant vigilance; and Fowler's work is a permanent warning.

The information is given in these short pithy paragraphs. The warnings are mainly conveyed in longer articles. It is really delightful to read them, for they combine lucid thinking with pungent expression, and at their best they have the same style and finish as a well-played game of chess. Very often Fowler gathers a large variety of roughly similar mistakes together under a common heading, disposes of them all in one article, and then has only to refer to it to convince his readers. To take an easy example, I suppose we all remember the phrase coined by a late President: *back to normalcy*. And I suppose most of us have felt uneasy about it, perhaps without knowing exactly why. *Normalcy* . . . it sounds wrong.

* See his article on the *Split Infinitive*.

Look it up in Fowler, and you will know what is wrong with it. He refers to his article on *Hybrid Derivatives*. Turn to that article. It begins:

> HYBRID DERIVATIVES are words formed from a stem or word belonging to one language by applying to it a suffix or prefix belonging to another. It will be convenient to class with these the words, abortions rather than hybrids, in which all the elements belong indeed to one language, but are so put together as to outrage that language's principles of formation . . . It will not be possible here to lay down rules for word-formation, which is a complicated business; but a few remarks on some of [these] words may perhaps instil caution, & a conviction that word-making, like other manufactures, should be done by those who know how to do it.

Well, that still does not tell us what is wrong with *back to normalcy*. But it shows us in which direction we should think. There is something wrong with the way the word is formed. *Normal* and *-cy* will not go together. Fowler does not tell us what is right—although a glance at the big Dictionary will show us. But he sets us to calculating. *Normalness?* No. *Normaltude?* No, no, no. But there is a formation which we do use: *abnormality*; and *formality*; and *legality*. That's it: *back to normality*.

There are two principles which govern language. One is usage: what most people say. The other is logic: what makes sense, what is consistent. Sometimes the two conflict, and then Fowler will use common sense and advise which we should follow. Often they agree, and then he will show us why. What he has—very briefly—shown us how to do is what we all do most of the time. Listen to two schoolboys talking about the behavior of a third. One will say, 'That's stupid. That's real stupidity!' The other will add, 'It's just plain dumbness'

—he won't say, 'dumbity.' The first will go on, 'It's just idiocy'
—not 'idiotness.' Sometimes he will say *idiotcy;* and then, if
he is wise, he will look up Fowler, who says

idiocy, -tcy. The *-t-* is wrong.*

Well, that is how Fowler works, and it is a pleasure to
watch him working. He had a pretty sure touch, because he
knew a great deal. He had an enormous store of information
about the English language which he had gathered while
working on the Dictionary. You see, what people sometimes
forget about language is that it exists not only in space but in
time. Spanish, for example, is not only the language which is
spoken from the Pyrenees to the Straits of Gibraltar and from
the Mexican frontier to Cape Horn (excepting Brazil and
some enclaves). It is also the language in which Cervantes
wrote his great novel and Góngora his astonishing pastoral
poems; and although these books were born in the seventeenth
century they are still alive, people still read them, they still
matter, they still affect the language quite as much as what
people say *now, in one district.* Similarly, when Fowler met a
problem in English, he asked himself not only what people
were saying in 1910 or 1920, but also what they had written
in the books which were still valid.

Here is a modern instance. During the last war the American government was putting out a phrase-book for soldiers
who were to occupy a foreign country. One of the phrases was
'I was laying on the bed.' The language experts objected, and
said that the correct American English was not that, but 'I
was lying on the bed.' The compilers of the book replied that
90 per cent of the GIs who would use the book always said,
'I was laying on the bed.'

Who was right?

---

* It is wrong because we don't say *vacantcy* or *advocatecy.*

Fowler states the facts first, as he knew them from his reading. *Lay* means 'put to rest,' *lie* means 'be at rest.' One is transitive, the other is intransitive. But then he adds, 'Confusion between the words *lay and lie* is very common in uneducated talk.'

In fact, broad usage—the custom of our language as represented in its books for centuries and in the speech of educated people always—says, 'I was lying on the bed.' But the temporary usage of this single group of speakers at one time says 'I was laying on the bed'; and since the Army book was being written only for that one purpose and time, it was right. Otherwise, wrong.

Fowler knew his historic English books well; he also knew contemporary writing well. He seems to have read all the daily and weekly papers and all the magazines, and to have clipped them for examples of good and bad writing. If he had put in only the horrors, the monstrous sentences which *The New Yorker* prints under headings like BLOCK THAT METAPHOR !, then his book would be rather painful to read. He really has some monsters, like this—

> Recognition is given to it by no matter whom it is displayed.

And this:

> Speculation on the subject of the constitution of the British representation at the Washington inauguration of the League of Nations . . .

But usually, when there is a problem, he not only prints what is wrong and analyzes it to show why it is wrong, but provides the alternative that should have been chosen. He does the work of a good copy editor, but explains it, too: for instance, take this sentence of gobbledygook:

As to how far such reinforcements are available, this is quite another matter.

Fowler says, 'omit "as to" and "this" ':

How far such reinforcements are available is quite another matter.

(He adds, 'The writer has chosen to get out of the room by a fire-escape when the door was open.')

There are not many people who can write such a level-headed book on a subject which they know very well, practice very effectively, and worry about. (Fortified by Mr. Fowler's defense of the habit, I have just ended a sentence with a preposition.)

He has his faults, as all strong writers and teachers have. His prejudices, however, are not irritating. In particular, he was not biased against American English. He realized that it was simply a different form, both in time and in space. He could scarcely foresee the present era, when the two languages —partly as a result of the last war, partly because of the movies and magazines, and partly also because of the sharing of experiences and modes of thought—are crossing each other's frontiers. I have heard my American friends using slang which I thought was purely English, and South-Eastern English at that; and I have seen bold Americanisms on the austere pages of the *Times Literary Supplement*.

Fowler's chief fault was that he did not realize how fertile a living language like English still is, and how it can be expanded, remade, revitalized by the effort of strongly imaginative people and adventurous talkers and writers. He lived too much alone, and too much with old books, and too much away from the ordinary working man, to know that. It would have done him good to spend a year in the Yorkshire factories, or in the deep South of the United States. He would have revised his views of the creative powers of our language if he had talked to the Negro mother who, when asked by the census-taker how old her children were, said: 'I has one lap baby, one crawler, one porch chile, and one yard young 'un.'

But his principal aim was not to encourage innovation, but to prevent degeneration and to promote flexibility, grace, and directness. Like Ernest Renan, he felt that a badly constructed sentence meant a badly formed thought, a truth ill conceived. He was not a creator. He was a teacher and a doctor. He loved our language when it was well spoken and well written. He hated the people who deform it by carelessness and ignorance: in the same way a doctor hates the men who pollute the public water supply or who sell decaying food. Therefore his book is really a draught of medicine—not sweet, not bitter, but astringent and cleansing. It is a good book because it is good for us, all of us, who speak, and write, and think.

———

H. W. Fowler, *A Dictionary of Modern English Usage* (Oxford, 1926, often reprinted; a revision is now being undertaken by the Press).
The *Balliol College Register*.
The Dictionary of National Biography.
G. G. Coulton, *Henry Fowler,* in S.P.E. Tract 43 (1934).

Science and Humanism: Sir William Osler

JUST over 30 years ago, in the then quiet and beautiful city of Oxford, there died an old gentleman with an olive-green face. He had suffered from catarrhal and bronchial infections all his life, and when he got his final attack of pneumonia he recognized it for what it used to be called, 'the old man's friend.' He was pretty strong, and he resisted it for weeks, until pleurisy and an influenza infection supervened. Then he knew it was over. He was a doctor himself, and when the physician in attendance tried to explain some of the symptoms, he said, 'You lunatic! I've been watching this case for two months, and I'm sorry I shall not do the post-mortem.' A few days later he was dead. But he left behind him the memory of a very odd and often very lovable character: something of it comes out in that remark, as it does in nearly everything he said and wrote. Recently I have been spending some time with him, in his own writings, and in a fine biography of him, written by a scientist who knew him well; and I should like to discuss his work and his character. He is no doubt watching us with an amused smile, and listening from some neighboring planet, and scribbling notes about us to his friend Sir Thomas Browne. His name is William Osler.

Osler was a Canadian, of Cornish descent. (That is where he got his peculiar appearance. Sargent, when he first saw him, said he had never before painted a man with a green complexion. His mother evidently belonged to one of the oldest groups in Britain, the pre-Celtic remnant which goes back beyond the Bronze Age: small, slender, wiry, dark, unpredictable, and sometimes dangerous.) He was born in 1849 on frontier territory in Upper Canada, where his father was a missionary. There were lots of Chippewa Indians around his birthplace, and one of them who saw the dark little baby lying in the cradle pointed at it and grunted, 'Papoose! Papoose!' As soon as he could walk he started getting into mischief, and he continued to do so all his life. Can you imagine the Regius Professor of Medicine at the University of Oxford, a dignitary some sixty years of age, standing in the lobby of the Athenaeum Club surreptitiously dropping heavy ashtrays into the pockets of other members while they read their mail? That was Osler in later life. As the twig is bent, so is the tree inclined.

He got a very good bad education at Trinity College School, near Toronto. I mean that he did not learn what he was expected to learn, and learned something else extremely well. The school was a new one, run by a solemn martinet who was trying to make it into a sort of Eton, or Charterhouse, or Arnold's Rugby. Nearly fifty years later, Osler remembered how stupidly and repulsively this man had taught them Greek and Latin. He and the other boys were full of energy, and were keen enough to learn: if they had been taught with imagination and humor—and without emphasis on the boring mechanics of language such as syntax and prosody—they would have turned out good classical scholars and writers. Even as it was, Osler retained a love for the classics throughout his long life. But although he was 'athirst for good literature,' he got only syntax and prosody. On the other hand, there was a scientist in the school, who could tell the boys about the stars, and take them on picnics where he showed them how the earth was made and where fossils came from, and with his microscope let them look at 'the marvels in a drop of dirty pond water.'

When he went on to Trinity College, Toronto, Osler was still not quite sure what he was going to be. His father had been a clergyman, and he was still thinking of theology. But he met another scientist, Bovell, who was a physiologist; and this decided him. You must have noticed how often a good teacher becomes a substitute father to his pupils, and although Osler was to become a greater man than Bovell, he remembered and revered him for the rest of his life. Many years afterward, when he was listening to a speech or attending a meeting, he would write his teacher's name and degrees again and again on the agenda-paper just as other people doodle a design: *James Bovell, M.D., M.R.C.P.,* again and again. It is very hard to become a great man without the influence of a good teacher.

In 1874 Osler became lecturer in medicine at McGill, and drew his first fee as a doctor: 'Speck in Cornea . . . 50¢.' At once he began to work with restless activity, revivifying the teaching of medicine, organizing medical societies, giving papers, and publishing the results of his own research. All his life he continued to be a terrific worker. For instance, in one year he did 100 autopsies. There are three large quarto volumes of notes on his observations, all written out in his own hand, numbered and indexed. And he taught with the same thoroughness. After the autopsies, he would display the specimens to his class, carefully correlating each of them with the history of the case (which the young men had already seen in hospital) and giving out written descriptions. One of his students says: 'There were always 4 pages and at times 8 pages of large letter size, written by himself and copied by means of a copying machine: there were from 30 to 40 copies required each Saturday, so that the demand such a task made on his time must have been heavy.'

Such a man was bound to succeed. Unless he was talking or walking or working in the lab, he rarely stopped reading; he nearly always took notes; and every year his knowledge—not only of Canadian and American but of German, English, and French medical discoveries—accumulated and deepened. Apparently he was not really a great discoverer: he worked out no new concepts and found no hitherto unsuspected secrets in the body: the single disease named after him, *polycythae-mia rubra*, had already been observed and described by another scientist. Rather he was a synthetist, a broad and copious mind who could contain and correlate hundreds of thousands of different facts which, perhaps, co-existed in the brains of only two or three other men throughout the world. Such a book is his one great work, *The Principles and Practice of Medicine*, for which he prepared during the years of his youth, which he wrote when he was forty-one, and which was such a success that he continued to produce new editions of it for the rest of his life. As well as learning, it was full of common sense, and of his own firmly held faith in nature as the chief healer. It is strange to hear him speak of the disease which killed him, and which now, Roger Lapham tells me, the doctor rarely sees:

> Pneumonia is a self-limited disease, and runs its course uninfluenced in any way by medicine. It can neither be aborted [nor be] cut short by any known means at our command.

But this came at a later stage of his career. In 1884, when he was thirty-five, he got his first Chair, and became Professor of Clinical Medicine at the University of Pennsylvania. He was by now acquiring a reputation as a consultant: he must have been admirable, for he never lacked sympathy and nearly always made a joke. (One of his patients was a white-haired, shaggy-bearded old man who lived at 328 Mickel Street, Camden, New Jersey, in a terrific litter of manuscripts, proof-sheets, and magazines and newspapers 'piled higher than the desk': his name was Mr. Walter Whitman, and he had written a book called *Leaves of Grass*.)

But the turning point in Osler's career came when he was appointed chief physician of the Johns Hopkins Hospital, in 1889, at the age of 40. He made it the first modern hospital in the United States. He also made it the first institution in America where students, instead of receiving more or less theoretical lectures about the character of disease, say the symptoms and probable course of dysentery, could stand around a patient actually suffering from dysentery, examine him, and if possible interrogate him, and thus begin their professional career as it was intended to continue, with an undeviating concentration on the patient who was to be cured. Further, Osler organized a remarkable staff, many of whom went on to become distinguished scientists; twice a month they met to read papers and discuss interesting cases, and perhaps once a month to review all the current medical periodicals from home and abroad. And Baltimore was a dirty city then, with no sewage system. Typhoid fever was endemic: Osler never tired of attacking the inferior sanitation of his new home, and in time the reforms were made, and the death rate began to drop.

Osler stayed at Johns Hopkins until he was nearly 60. He had married immediately after finishing his textbook, and had begotten one son. These were really the busiest and best years of his life. But he determined to retire at sixty, for as he advanced in his profession, money and honors flowed in upon him, and he felt very strongly—perhaps too strongly—that after middle life a man's usefulness decreases very rapidly. In 1905 he got an unexpected honor—which it was difficult to refuse, partly because he was anxious to retire but not to drop out altogether, and partly because he had always loved Europe and particularly England. He was offered, and accepted, the Regius Professorship of Medicine at Oxford University.

An odd thing happened to him as he left Baltimore. I said a little earlier that he was dangerous and unpredictable. Well, his tongue ran away with him. He gave a farewell address in the great hall of Johns Hopkins, and in it, explaining that men were useless—commercially, politically, and professionally—after sixty, he mentioned a novel by Anthony Trollope in which death by chloroform at sixty-one is recommended. He went on to say (no doubt with a pleasant smile) that 'incalculable benefits might follow such a scheme.' Next day the storm broke. The newspapers cried OSLER RECOMMENDS CHLOROFORM AT SIXTY. Truckloads of abusive letters poured in on him (to be diverted and destroyed by his secretary) and there were many hundreds of newspaper clippings, nearly all hostile. It was a hard punishment for indiscretion. If he had been a coldhearted scientist, whose only interest was efficiency, the remark would have been more explicable, and his reaction to the public indignation would have been firmer. But he had always had a warm heart; he was particularly kind to the old and the suffering. He had simply allowed himself, as he did from time to time, to be dominated by the Imp of the Perverse.

The scientists, I think, will say that his career really ended when he went to Oxford. They may be right, if they mean his career as a scientist. He did not manage to organize a complete medical school at Oxford: the city was not large enough, the hospitals were not suitable, London was too near, the colleges were not designed for such a thing, there were other claims on his time, and perhaps he was too tired. Perhaps it was not necessary. But his career expanded, and he fulfilled himself, in other ways. He now became not only a scientist, but, as he had always been in embryo, a humanist. He had always collected books about the history of science; now he became a curator of the Bodleian Library and gave an enormous impetus to the Library in its acquisition of these rare and valuable works, many of which he himself presented to it. He had always taught the young men that they should be fully alive human beings, as well as healers and discoverers; and he had always driven this lesson home to them by describing the lives of great doctors of the past. Now he wrote delightful essays and delivered humane lectures on his predecessors: Servetus, who discovered the secondary circulation and was burnt alive by Calvin; Burton, the anatomist of melancholy; Harvey; Browne; Patin; and others, all his eternal colleagues and his friends.

This is chiefly what people love about Osler: his ability to show the world that science is not a dehumanized activity carried out by calculating machines, but the work of live men devoted to the cause of better life; his strong sense that research is part of the general and broader activity of learning, teaching, and public information; his belief that science is only one part of the life of a scholar, however great a discoverer he may be, and that the appreciation of literature and, even more genuinely, the enjoyment of life, humor, and friendship are the better part, without which the investigator is a monk walling himself into his own cell and closing the windows.

Was he happy? I suppose he was; and successful. Yet I sometimes feel sad when I read his life. Very few of us are harmonious. Osler was not, and through his life there is a persistent sour note. He lived like Prokofieff's music: you know that angular excitement which is so seldom calm and rich, always so effortful. The worst of it is that he had only one son, who was killed in the First World War (like Kipling's): that killed him, too. Even his jokes sometimes turned sour—as when he told the graduating nurses at Hopkins, after their long and devoted training, that nurses were only an added horror for the sick man, who merely wanted to turn his face to the wall 'and, if he so wishes, die undisturbed.' He couldn't stand practical jokes against himself, and the few which were tried fell flat or hurt him. He was one of the few distinguished men of letters and science who have had a double personality: he called himself Egerton Y. Davis of Caughnawauga, and would tell stories about Davis's life and discoveries to comparative strangers, and sign the name in hotel registers. Can we understand this? I think so. The middle name, the Y, was Yorrick—which was of course a pseudonym of Laurence Sterne, in whom Osler was deeply interested. And one of Sterne's chief models was another doctor, who closely resembled Osler: François Rabelais, an investigator, though not a palmary discoverer; a joker; a writer; and a universal man. This is Osler's real ancestry. Osler was one of the doctors who love humanity so much that they strive all their lives to alleviate suffering and to teach others to do the same; and meanwhile they laugh, almost *too* wildly and dangerously, because laughter is liveliness, and both the scholar and the doctor are engaged in preserving and intensifying life.

H. Cushing, *The Life of Sir William Osler* (Oxford University Press, 1940).

W. Osler, *The Principles and Practice of Medicine* (16th edition, ed. H. A. Christian, Appleton-Century-Crofts, 1947).

W. Osler, *Selected Writings* (Oxford, 1948).

An American Poet

IT is sad that the word *romantic* has been so misused and vulgarized. If it had not been, we could call this American poet a romantic figure. Most of the many meanings implied in the word would fit him: unorthodox, strongly individual, imaginative and emotional, daring, careless of routine success, a lover only of the material things which can be loved without desire (not money and machines, but mountains, waters, birds, animals); lonely, too, lonely. Yes, he is a romantic figure.

His name is Robinson Jeffers. He lives in Carmel, California, in a house which he and his sons built, stone by stone. He is getting on toward seventy now. When he first settled in Carmel, it was a small windswept village smelling of trees and the sea, inconveniently simple, unfrequented, unfashionable, a good place for a man to be himself and nobody else.

Now—at least in the summer—it is a bright and busy seaside town, with a beach, cocktail bars, branches of very chi-chi metropolitan stores, and a rich flow of traffic from the rest of California. Why, in those quaint narrow streets there is hardly room for all the Cadillacs. This is the same kind of change which, in our own lifetime, has infected many other places: Montauk, Acapulco, Oxford, Provincetown, you can fill out the list yourselves. Mr. Jeffers does not enjoy the change. He did not expect it when he built his home there on the lonely peninsula near Point Lobos. But he is a pessimist, and he has long been convinced that mankind spoils nearly everything it touches. He does not, therefore, see much of the beauties of prosperous California. He prefers to watch the ocean which is full of life but which is too cold and powerful for us to swim in, the rocky hills which will not grow grapefruit, but have a superhuman dignity of their own.

Mr. Jeffers is not a popular poet. He never wished to be a popular poet, he has shunned every device which leads toward popularity, he avoids publicity, he will not lecture and give readings and play the guitar, he has no immediate disciples, and has formed no school. It is not that he is deliberately obscure. You can understand all his poetry, if you read it with care: far more easily than the work of his contemporaries Eliot and Pound and Valéry. It is not that he was once ambitious, and is now soured by lack of recognition: far from it. His poetry is not meant to be liked. It is meant, I think, to do people good.

But it is very remarkable poetry, and he is a very distinguished man. America has produced great statesmen, soldiers, engineers, explorers, civilizers, inventors, and actors. It has produced—in nearly two centuries—very few great poets. Robinson Jeffers may prove to be one of those great poets. I say *may*, because I honestly do not know whether he will or not. But if he does, he will be like some other solitary artists who were recognized during their lives as odd, provocative, masterful, self-sufficient, and eccentric; and whose work turned out to be as durable as stone. Such was Euripides, whom Mr. Jeffers admires and something resembles; such was Lucretius; such was Dante; such were Breughel, and Monteverdi, and Poe. It takes time . . . it takes at least a century for a good work of poetry to prove what it is.

If you have not read Mr. Jeffers' poems, there is a handsome one-volume edition of his *Selected Poetry*. When you look over it, what you will see is this: a single, comparatively small book about 600 pages in all. Not much for a life's work, you may think; but many of these poems are the result of thirty or forty years of thought, and they are intended to live ten times, or a hundred times, as long.

You will see that Mr. Jeffers writes three different types of poem. Some are meditative lyrics, anywhere between ten and forty lines long—a thought, a brief description of something seen, a memory or a vision. Some are long narrative poems—that is a good form which we are foolish to neglect nowadays: a story told in verse is harder to do, but often far more effective, than a story told in prose. There are about a dozen exciting, lurid, visionary narrative poems set in the wild hill-country of central California near Monterey. They are about bitter loves, and hatreds more satisfying than love. Crime, sensuality, madness haunt them. Brothers kill each other. Fearful illicit passions rage through them like forest fires.

In the same form Mr. Jeffers has also written several dramas, and poems partly narrative and partly dramatic, most of them on plots from Greek tragedy. The best known is his adaptation of the *Medea,* which was (he says himself) inspired by Judith Anderson's art and personality, and which showed us her magnificent acting in New York during the winter of 1947-8. These, pieces also move among the grim ideas which have long filled his mind and which are the basis of his poetry.

Both the lyrics and the stories are written in large, muscular, unrhymed lines, with an irregular pulse which is basically a new sort of blank verse, with a long rhythm (about ten beats to the line) which reminds me irresistibly of the Pacific hammering at the rocks. It is intended to echo the ebb and flow of excitement, the interchange of narrative and speech. For my taste it is usually too irregular, because I can remember poetry only when it has a fairly steady pattern; still, it is free and powerful and eloquent, anything but monotonous and conventional.

Now, if I try to explain what Mr. Jeffers' themes are, I shall risk distorting them, oversimplifying them, making them too naïve or brutal, breaking up their subtle interrelations, vulgarizing a poetic statement by changing it into a Message. And yet his work is very cohesive, so that one can bring out its leading motives, as one could not do with a wayward poet like Yeats; and his ideas are so strange that unless we are boldly introduced to them, we may not comprehend them at all. He is a tragic poet; and tragedy is a truth which is hard, hard to understand.

First, let us look at one of his short poems. Through it we can see his manner and a few of his leading thoughts. It is called 'Summer Holiday.'

> When the sun shouts and people abound
> One thinks there were the ages of stone and the age of
>   bronze
> And the iron age; iron the unstable metal;
> Steel made of iron, unstable as his mother; the towered-
>   up cities
> Will be stains of rust on mounds of plaster.

Roots will not pierce the heaps for a time, kind rains
  will cure them,
Then nothing will remain of the iron age
And all these people but a thigh-bone or so, a poem
Stuck in the world's thought, splinters of glass
In the rubbish dumps, a concrete dam far off in the
  mountain . . .

Now, there is no sex in this, while there is a great deal in Mr.
Jeffers' long poems. There is no clash of personalities, while
his major works are boldly dramatic. But the strong pessimism
is characteristic; so is the sense of history; so is the peculiar
blend of deep, long thought and deeply felt but controlled
emotion; so is the sense of the earth—our mother, our home,
and our grave.

You may not think this an attractive poem. But you will
agree it is memorable. You will remember it. Through remembering it, you may come to admire it, and to understand
more of an eminent but deliberately isolated American writer.

Mr. Jeffers, you see, believes a number of terrible things.
They are not all true for Christians, who believe in redemp-
tion; but they are true for many other inhabitants of this
world.

First, he believes that men and women are animals. For
him, there is *no difference* between a delicatessen, or a fur
store, and a pack of coyotes hunting down a deer . . . except
that the coyotes hunt and devour in hot blood, whereas we
breed the meat-cattle and slaughter them and trap the furry
animals and skin them with a cold greedy purposefulness
which is more disgusting. Many animals are cruel and noble.
Their cruelty contains style and courage, the cougar and the
hawk. Men and women are usually cruel. When they are
cruel and mean, they are loathsome . . . animals. When they
are cruel and noble, they may be noble animals.

Then, Mr. Jeffers utterly abominates war, modern war. He sees it as a symptom and a cause of what he considers the decadence of our civilization. He believes that growing populations and multiplying machines all over the world have distorted the balance of nature, and that war is now the greatest of all such distortions. His last book was full of violent isolationism. One might expect him to regard the whole of warfare as an understandable activity like the ferocity of animals: to think of the shark when he sees a submarine, to admire the flight of bombers as much as the flight of the hawks; but he cannot.

Third, he is unlike most of us in his view of happiness. Most people, I think he would say, want easy pleasure and drowsy happiness. But real fulfillment is not pleasure: it is something more powerful. Effort and suffering are more natural than rest and enjoyment. Pain lasts longer and is more real than pleasure.

Fourth—the fourth of Mr. Jeffers' themes is the grandest of all, and the most wretched, and the most difficult. It is this. *The human race is not needed.* It is an infestation from which the planet is suffering. Look at a wooded mountainside, with the bear and the deer in the forests, the badger and the fox in the brush, birds and their cousins the reptiles crawling and flying above and below. Can you truthfully say that it would improve that scene to drive a six-lane motor-highway across it? Or to put a town in the middle of it? And when people say that it would be a terrific disaster if another war blotted out the human race, do they mean it? Do they mean that the mountains would weep, the rivers run backward with grief, and the animals and the birds go into mourning? Or would the earth begin its peaceful work of purification, covering up —with falling leaves and drifting dust and sifting earth and growing plants and moving hillsides and encroaching forests—

our cities, our factories, and our prisons? And then would the whole planet, with its other children, heave a single, long, unanimous sigh of relief?

These are some of the ideas which—unless I have gravely misunderstood him—Robinson Jeffers holds. He also has an extremely complex and difficult conception of sex, and the family, as a source of tragedy. He has made these themes into fine poetry. He does not think they are pleasant ideas. But he thinks they are true. He thinks that they have the truth of nature; that they are somehow part of nature. And he loves nature, wild nature. In this he is more like a primitive American than a modern man—like the Indian who climbed Chief Mountain to be alone and see visions, or the early white hunters who went west because they loved land and animals without humanity. But he is also like several distinguished American artists: Thoreau; Melville; Martha Graham, and Ernest Hemingway. Most of nature, he knows, is not pleasant; but it is—well, what is a thunderstorm? What is a forest fire? What is a north wind bringing bitter snow over the mountains? or the ocean surging against a rocky cliff? The sound, the power, the terror, and the nobility of these things make the truth of Robinson Jeffers' poetry.

———

R. Jeffers, *Selected Poetry* (Random House, 1938).

The Criticism of Edmund Wilson

W<small>E</small> are going to discuss Edmund Wilson as a critic; and indeed he is a distinguished critic. But he is more than that. He is also a dramatist: his play, *The Little Blue Light,* was produced in 1951 before perplexed but interested audiences. He is an ingenious poet, and has published a long poem (*The Pickerel Pond*) in an unusual form—couplets with reverse rhymes, where *reed* rhymes to *deer* and *pines* to *snipe.* He is an interesting and sometimes shocking storyteller—you recall his *Memoirs of Hecate County.* He has issued several difficult but rewarding essays on politics. And one of the things I like best about him is that he is a humorist. Most critics are preternaturally solemn. They get discouraged by reading masses and masses of print, searching for talent in mountains of clay and ink; they exhaust themselves trying to work out principles; sometimes, if they try to remain too long on a very lofty spiritual level, they suffer from lack of oxygen, and get the intellectual 'bends.' But Wilson really likes books; he usually keeps his feet on the ground; and does not take himself or literature too seriously, so that he has nearly always been able to see the funny side. One or two of the stories in *Hecate County* were wildly comical; and when he takes to parody, everybody laughs except the victim. Listen to him on the admirers of Franz Kafka (this is from a dream-poem, *The Mass in the Parking Lot,* privately published a year or two ago):

> With a rumble-de-bum and a pifka-pafka
> Came the fife-and-drum corps parading for Kafka.

(It sounds like *Hary Janos,* doesn't it?)

> Full of multiple meanings and *sotto voce's,*
> They had more and more grown to resemble roaches:
> Thus debasing themselves, they grew close to the
>   Master,
> And could crawl into cracks to avoid disaster.

Parody is itself a form of criticism: and an effective one. And although Wilson can do many different things—indeed, one never knows what he will do next—the main body of his work is criticism of literature. Let us look it over.

He was born in 1895, and went to Princeton. There he belonged to an important generation, one which produced several interesting men: among them Scott Fitzgerald, whom Wilson knew and liked. He learned a great deal from Princeton, particularly from Christian Gauss, to whom he has paid an eloquent tribute in his latest book, *The Shores of Light.* After graduating he served in World War I, and then became a journalist—which in a sense he still is. He worked on *Vanity Fair* and on the editorial staff of *The New Republic.*

At some time in the 'twenties he became interested in socialism. Since he is an intelligent man, it did not take him too long to see that Marxism is the opium of the intellectuals, and that the dictatorship of one party is bound to mean tyranny, cruelty, and the exercise of 'power for the sake of power.' In this he is to be compared with George Orwell, Arthur Koestler, André Malraux, and André Gide—although, unlike most of them, he remains an optimist with a limited but secure faith in the human race. He likes the Russians as people, and he despises the cold doctrinaires and the cunning despots who control them. The result is that he has been given the treatment reserved for writers whom the Communists have blacklisted: venomous attacks on his private and public life have been put about by the party's ruthless hatchetmen, and when not vilified he has been ostentatiously ignored. But these detestable tactics are by now becoming well known. Wilson has treated them with contempt, and will survive them.

In 1931 he published the work which established his reputation. This was *Axel's Castle*. It was the first book to explain the poetry of Yeats, Eliot, and Valéry, and the prose of Proust, Joyce, and Stein, together with the careers of other oddities like Rimbaud. The book was a revelation to young men interested in literature. It brought contemporary literature really into focus for many of us who, when reading *transition,* had been bewitched, but also bothered and bewildered. The title of the book is not merely fanciful. Axel is the hero of a crazy and wonderful play by Villiers de l'Isle Adam, who, when offered everything that life can give (love, beauty, wealth, power), turns his back on it and chooses death, because the ideal is superior to the real. In the same way, Wilson suggests, writers like Valéry and the early Eliot and the deliberately unintelligible Stein shrank from life—fearing it, or hating it.

Some years later, in 1938, Wilson produced *The Triple Thinkers* (the title comes from a phrase of Flaubert): a collection of essays which contains some really hard thinking about Henry James, Bernard Shaw, Pushkin, and A. E. Housman. (I should add here that he is one of the few modern critics who know the Greek and Latin classics in the original, and are well acquainted with standards which were not invented yesterday by one group or nation, but reflect the artistic expression and thought of 3000 years.)

In 1941 appeared a short set of his essays on the California school, the group composed of Saroyan, Steinbeck, James Cain, and one or two more. Like some other visitors to the West Coast, Wilson has been impressed by its unreality: the fact that it appears (apart from San Francisco) to have no real structure, roots, relations, no purpose except to have a Good Time. He calls it 'the Pacific vacuum.' Evidently he still recalls with sorrow the ruin of Scott Fitzgerald, who, like others, found his talents wasted and his weakness emphasized by that El Dorado, where gold streams down in the rays of the generous, gushing, unselective sun. Here again Wilson touched one of the central themes of his thought: the link between the writer and contemporary life. The writer must know it and feel it, and yet stand apart in order to interpret it.

In the same year, 1941, he issued a much bigger book, *The Wound and the Bow.* (Like most of his work, it is a collection of essays previously published. He uses magazines as Churchill uses page proofs, making them a final test for the harmony of his prose and the precision of his thought: he revises carefully, and republishes only after long consideration.) This is a collection of spacious studies of some interesting writers: Kipling and Dickens, both shown, not as normal, straightforward, rather superficial authors, but (more penetratingly) as neurotics urged on by passions, thoughts, and fears they themselves scarcely dared to face. Edith Wharton and Hemingway also appear; both are shown as mastered by, or striving to master, terrible inner conflicts. Joyce's new *Finnegans Wake* (which very few critics dare to discuss at length) is analyzed; Casanova, whom hardly anyone treats as a serious writer, is portrayed both as a writer and as a man; and a Greek tragedy by Sophocles is examined, with illustrative quotations in Greek. This is not a piece of show-off or pedantry: the essay ties the whole book together. Its theme is the strange tragic plot of *Philoctetes*, in which a soldier, wounded, poisoned, and marooned by his comrades, is discovered to be essential to the purpose of the army which deserted him. He is ill, but indispensable.

In this peculiar situation Wilson sees reflected the position of the artist—not only in our own time but throughout history. I don't know if he is right. Neither does he. Artists may be fascinating eccentrics, like Robert Burton; or dangerous screwballs, like Lautréamont; or devil-worshippers like the Marquis de Sade, who hate the human race and would like to pull its wings off and poke out its eyes; or vulgar exhibitionists like D'Annunzio. The relation of the artist to society is a very complex thing, changing with every change in the social structure; and one of the certainties which his knowledge of other times and other countries has brought to Edmund Wilson is the realization that no single formula, political or economic or even aesthetic, will explain it.

Since then, the best of his critical work has been collected in two volumes, *Classics and Commercials* (1950) and *The Shores of Light* (1952). The former is largely composed of his articles published recently in *The New Yorker,* and the latter of his reviews written during the 'twenties and 'thirties for *The New Republic*. Their range is astonishingly wide. I cannot think of any other critic who would be capable of writing intelligently about Faulkner, Sartre, Tolstoy, and Shakespeare, about such eccentricities as manuals of conjuring and the biography of Houdini, about both burlesque shows and Emily Post, about both best sellers and obscure difficult authors, and—here is a peculiar and rather touching specialty of Wilson's—about about interesting near-failures like John Jay Chapman. There is almost too much in these books. Wilson himself says that it is difficult to be a journalist living on your earnings, and also to be a serious critic.

> To write what you are interested in writing and to suc-
> ceed in getting editors to pay for it, is a feat that may
> require pretty close calculation and a good deal of
> ingenuity . . . You have to develop a resourcefulness at
> pursuing a line of thought through pieces on miscel-
> laneous and more or less fortuitous subjects; and you
> have to acquire a technique of slipping over on the
> routine of editors the deeper independent work which
> their over-anxious intentness on the fashions of the
> month or the week has conditioned them automatically
> to reject, as the machines that make motor parts auto-
> matically reject outsizes.*

Difficult: yes, it is difficult for others; but it has become easier for him. He writes about so many things because he has a multitude of active and growing ideas, and because he chooses the new intellectual experiences that will feed them. I hope that the result of all this activity will be a work of literary criticism which is more closely woven and structurally more complete.

But even if it is not, his work will continue to be vitally interesting. He says himself that he most admires three journalist-critics: De Quincey, Poe, and Shaw. In his own line, I think he is better than all of them. I should rather

---

* *Classics and Commercials*, p. 112.

parallel him to a man who had a career, and perhaps a character, not unlike his own: a settled romantic, a poet and novelist, a well-trained classicist, an omnivorous reader, a sociable epicure and also a withdrawn thinker; a man who sat at a café table almost every week for years, looking at the spectacle of life and criticizing it as interpreted by literature; and—although it is not easy to evoke any single set of Principles from his work—a critic who is always worth reading, even when you have not read the book he is discussing and do not know the subject. This is Charles-Augustin Sainte-Beuve: whose regular Monday articles, published in a huge collection of twenty-eight volumes, make wonderful reading when you are devoid of ideas, or simply distrustful of the human intelligence.

That is the best thing about Edmund Wilson as a critic. He believes in the mind, and the taste, and the fancy. He dislikes the tyrants who try to throttle them or starve them or exploit them, and he enjoys every activity which sends blood through them, lets them expand, gives them hope and laughter, precision and purpose. I gather he is now working on a survey of American literature during the two powerful generations between 1870 and 1910 . . . a difficult and important theme, the growth and education of a young giant. It is a subject well worthy of his imagination, his penetration, his style, and his patriotism. I look forward with great pleasure to reading it, and meanwhile I thank him for all the stimulus he has given me in the past twenty years.

Look, we have just completed a discussion of an eminent critic without once using the word *integrity*. This feat was very difficult, and (as Cocteau says in the prologue to *Orphée*) 'carried out entirely without safety-nets.' But seriously, it was an attempt to follow Wilson's own pattern, and to talk about interesting books and important subjects without using the private and sometimes unintelligible language which implies that the Best is for the Few. Edmund Wilson does not believe that. He believes, I think, that the best is for us all—if we will use our minds, and resist the tempters, both the cruel and the kind.

Edmund Wilson, *Axel's Castle* (Scribner, 1931 and 1950).
The Boys in the Back Room (Colt Press, 1941).
Classics and Commercials (Farrar, Straus, 1950).
The Little Blue Light (Farrar, Straus, 1950).
Memoirs of Hecate County (Doubleday, 1946).
The Shores of Light (Farrar, Straus, 1952).
The Triple Thinkers (Harcourt, Brace, 1938; Oxford University Press, 1948).
The Wound and the Bow (Houghton Mifflin, 1941; Oxford University Press, 1947).

Lawrence in America

Really he is an unforgettable character, even to us who never saw him. We know him partly through the descriptions given by his admirers and his enemies, partly through pictures, and partly through the projections of himself in his books. There he is, the small thin man with the beard which meant so many things: a disguise; an artist's costume; the mask of Pan; the face of the Saviour. His wanderings through the world, we know them, too, and how he pushed on, restless and yet not unhappy, an explorer rather than an exile. His paintings, so bold and crude, but vital. His poems, so corny but occasionally so charming, like a schoolboy's. His prose style, which was so strong and lasting when he worked at it with passion, and so shrill and trivial when he tore at it with excitement. He himself would have distinguished passion and excitement in life (particularly in sexual life); but he could not always distinguish them in art.

Or else, to put it more kindly, Lawrence was a weak and ill and undereducated man with a rickety and badly strained character, who tried all his life to make himself into a strong and healthy and deeply cultured man with a profound calm possession of himself and of the world. He partly succeeded. But he had to go on struggling all his life. We see him in constant struggle and constant change. He is hard to see consistently; but he is impossible to forget.

A recent selection of his work shows us some of these struggles. This is *The Later D. H. Lawrence,* published by Knopf. Beautifully printed and bound, like all Borzoi books, it has highly percipient introductions and notes by the chief guide through the Laurentian Mountains, William York Tindall. It is full of good reading, mixed with some outstandingly bad reading; yet always vital reading. You may be annoyed or disgusted, but you don't lose interest.

When Lawrence was forty-four, he left England for good. The rest of his life he spent trying to get warm—in countries like Mexico and Italy, which can sometimes be deathly cold, but heat up in the summer at least. A new period of his life began. He had eleven years to live; and in them, he talked a great deal, he traveled a great deal, and he did an astounding amount of work.

Until then he had thought mainly about England and its complicated social structure. (He never really stopped thinking in social terms: he would arrange people in a hierarchy: peasants and priests and chiefs; or inert people near the soil, more intense people who rode horses, and rich owners of land who were dying or dead.) But from then on he found it harder to use English society as a general framework for his ideas. So much of it is placid; and Lawrence hated placidity. So much of it is superficial; and Lawrence loved penetration. So much of it is slightly comic; and Lawrence loved the lyric, the heroic, and the tragic.

Also, until this period of his life, he had been thinking mainly about the problems of the conventional novel—the complex plot, the well-assorted characters, the descriptions and the conversations and the climaxes. Into this he had kept trying to pour a flood of symbols and strange evocations and products of the unconscious, which very often threatened to break out of the framework and make it a mass of meaningless fragments. From then on he began to communicate in many different mediums: meditative essays, long short stories (alas, that splendid form, how it suffers from having no title, only that miserable sticky Italian label, the *novella*!), paintings, poems, addresses to the public in the manner of Nietzsche, and descriptions of important scenes experienced while he traveled.

This selection begins with a novel, which is really almost a total failure. It is called *St. Mawr*. Roughly, it is the story of two American women. They try living in England. The daughter marries Sir Henry Carrington. Sir Henry buys a stallion—or rather his wife buys a stallion—which throws him and makes him an invalid. The women sympathize with the horse. They take it to America, leaving Sir Henry in bed, with an affectionate caretaker. They roam for a while. The mother proposes to a Welsh groom, who refuses her. The daughter thinks about proposing to a Mexican-Indian groom (preparation for *Lady Chatterley*). Then the two women buy a ranch outside Santa Fe. There, suddenly, the story stops.

We hear no more of the stallion, or of the grooms; we do not know what kind of life these two spoiled women are going to have there, on a remote hillside in New Mexico. The daughter talks about it in that peculiar rhetoric which infuriates some people when they read Lawrence, and which affects others rather like drums beating, urgent but meaningless, non-intellectual but important. She says:

> There's something . . . that loves me and wants me. I can't tell you what it is. It's a spirit. And it's here, on this ranch. It's here, in this landscape. It's something more real to me than men are, and it soothes me, and it holds me up . . . I am here, right deep in America, where there's a wild spirit wants me, a wild spirit more than men . . .

Fantastic, isn't it? Yet not silly. Compared with the landscape of New Mexico, the social life of dear little Winter Overcotes and even the social life of London itself look very thin, they are soon outworn, they are restful but not sustaining. The novel is like that. It has many things in it which are fantastic, but not silly. Still, it is a failure.

Yet interesting, too. Its chief interest is that it shows us a man trying hard to do something quite new and important. Lawrence can no longer concern himself with the conversations which make up so much of the shared life of people in the same social class. He either writes brief cryptic exchanges between people so different that they can scarcely communicate, or else creates monologues within the minds of his characters and himself. He is less and less interested in the ordinary persons who make up the entire world of such novelists as Balzac and Proust and Dostoevsky; more and more in those other beings who occupy most of this planet—peasants who dislike talk, natives who communicate almost without talk,

grooms who are partly animal, and animals who are as in-
tensely alive as human beings. Lawrence thought a great deal
about our fellow creatures who cannot speak, and one of his
chief aims was to understand how they lived without the
burden of thought and the constriction of speech. They live
as richly as we do: more so; or not much less so; but how do
they live? And what is their real relation to us? What is the
link between a man and a horse? between a man and his
dog? between a man and the wolf he shoots? How can we
share the same world as a snake, without either hating it or
ignoring it? There is a fine piece about the Hopi Snake Dance,
in which, as few others could do, Lawrence really shows how
venomous reptiles can co-exist with human beings, and be in
their own way beautiful, and perhaps share an experience.
Here is one sentence describing the sight which makes all the
tourists squirm. It does not make us squirm. It makes us
thoughtful and tranquil.

> A young priest emerged, bowing reverently, with the
> neck of a pale, delicate rattlesnake held between his
> teeth, the little, naïve, bird-like head of the rattlesnake
> quite still, near the black cheek, and the long, pale,
> yellowish, spangled body of the snake dangling like
> some thick, beautiful cord.

Who else would have thought of calling a rattlesnake delicate? Or calling its head birdlike? or, still more, naïve? Who
else would have noticed that the hanging body of the snake
—which to most of us is so frightening in motion and so repulsive in repose—was decorative, 'like some thick, beautiful
cord'?

And later, in a very silly book called *The Man Who Died,*
there appears one of the commonest and silliest of non-human
characters, the barnyard rooster—who is nevertheless described

with humorous sympathy and pathetic understanding, not for intelligence and a sense of purpose and other things which he does not possess (except in Rostand's *Chantecler*), but for his pluck and silliness and flamboyant good looks. That kind of thing can be done by a good artist in music (you remember the warning cry in Rimsky-Korsakov's *Golden Cock*), and by a good plastic artist, a sculptor like Jacques Lipchitz or an Oriental potter; but it is amazingly hard to do it in prose.

In this effort to understand animals and to sympathize with them, without humanizing them, I think Lawrence was more English than he knew. Compare him with Thoreau and Whitman, who, although they loved all living things, did not care particularly about animals, and who wrote little about the peculiar process of understanding them; and then compare him with such English writers as T. H. White, who has published an extraordinary book about training a half-wild goshawk; or Peter Scott the bird-watcher; or Jim Corbett the hunter; or Gerard Manley Hopkins the poetic visionary.

And perhaps Lawrence always remained the Englishman, even when he thought of himself as quite detached from England. The next 130 pages in this collection contain essays on life in the Southwest of the United States and in Mexico. Throughout them, Lawrence is obviously trying very hard to understand the Indians and the Mexicans and the country where they live, without assimilating them all to his own culture, telling them what they ought to do, establishing his own superiority to them, or sympathizing with their backwardness. More travelers from England have done that than travelers from any other Western nation. Think of T. E. Lawrence and the Arabs; of Joyce Cary and the West Africans; of E. M. Forster and the Hindu and the Moslem; of Doughty and the Arabs, in that marvelous book *Arabia Deserta*; and, to go farther back, of Browning and the Italians, or Byron and the

Greeks. Within that tradition I have seldom read anything better than Lawrence's reflections upon Indian dancing. Consider this:

> There is [for the Indian] strictly no god. The Indian does not consider himself as created, and therefore external to God, or the creature of God. To the Indian there is no conception of a defined God. Creation is a great flood, forever flowing, in lovely and terrible waves. In everything, the shimmer of creation, and never the finality of the created. Never the distinction between God and God's creation, or between Spirit and Matter. Everything, everything is the wonderful shimmer of creation, it may be a deadly shimmer like lightning or the anger in the little eyes of the bears, it may be the beautiful shimmer of the moving deer, or the pine boughs softly swaying under snow . . . All is godly.

Now, I don't know whether this is true or not. Oliver La Farge, who has written such wonderful spiritual reconstructions of Navajo life, and Frank Waters, who knows the languages and has come as near to the Indian mysteries as any living white man, might say that, for the Indians, there are gods, though not a God; and they might add that Lawrence here sounds too much like a Western pantheist and too little like an interpreter of the Indian spirit. What I myself have tried to understand of the Navajo rites of healing, centering upon their beautiful religious paintings, makes me think that there is, for them, a sharp difference between spirit and matter, human and superhuman, evil and good, kindly and malevolent; and that their cosmos is symmetrical like a hogan, not fluid like a river. But Lawrence was thinking chiefly of the Pueblo Indians, and perhaps he was right about them. And in any case he was sympathetic and eloquent: we can ask no more.

Some authors spend their entire lives trying to justify. They will write novel after novel, play after play, to prove that they were right when they ran away from home, or deserted their first husband. Others spend all their lives remembering, going back and back over the experiences of the first twenty-five years, interpreting and reinterpreting as though nothing had happened since then, and as though the initial pattern were the final one. Lawrence was a rarer type, for he spent his life in trying to understand; and, very often, when he had understood one group of people, he would go elsewhere to meet others and try to understand them. To meet, to understand, to love, and then—to leave . . .

He was a spiritual Don Juan, and his fugitive beloved was the entire human race.

———

The Later D. H. Lawrence (ed. W. Y. Tindall, Knopf, 1952).

Poetry and Romance: John Masefield

ABOUT twenty years ago, when I went to college, I had a room right at the top of the tower in the front quadrangle. (I remember it had about ninety steps up to it, and of course no elevator, so that it was awkward if I got down to go to a lecture and then found I had forgotten my books.) There were a lot of good pianists in college then, and on a fine evening with the windows open you could usually hear two or three pianos going at once. Some of the best music, best played, used to come from a room almost directly beneath mine—all the things I liked but couldn't manage to play myself, Albeniz and the Chopin studies, plus a number of things I had never heard, like Bartok's Roumanian Dances. In due course, I got to know the young fellow who lived there and played so well. He was Lewis Masefield, son of John

Masefield, the Poet Laureate. He is dead now: he was killed in the war; but during the years we were at college I got to know him quite well. He was a sensitive youngster, with beautiful taste: he would have become a fine artist.

Well, partly because of that, and partly because of some poetry I had been publishing in magazines, I was invited out to Boars Hill to meet the Poet Laureate himself. I was a bit overawed; but in time I got to know Mr. Masefield and Mrs. Masefield a little better. They are both charming people, and they were exceedingly kind to me. I haven't seen them for a long time now, but recently I have been reading Mr. Masefield's autobiographical book, *So Long To Learn,* and it has set me to thinking about him and his work.

When I first went out to Boars Hill, I thought of John Masefield only in the way that I suppose most of us think of him: as the poet of the sea. Everyone knows his song, 'Sea-Fever':

> I must go down to the seas again, to the lonely sea and
> the sky;
> And all I ask is a tall ship, and a star to steer her by.

That is one of several sea-pieces which we all know and like. Besides those, I knew he had published half a dozen spanking adventure stories, in very good, carefully written, and easily read prose. And I knew he had first won his reputation by composing several long poems which (in the years before 1914) seemed very shocking, because they were about turbulent passions and violent crimes, because their characters were ordinary people (poachers and farmers and vagrants) yet lived more intense lives than ladies and gentlemen, and because they contained brutal oaths and slang and everyday language, mixed up with their poety. I remembered hearing about these poems, and looking into one or two of them; but they were out of fashion in the 1920's and 1930's, when we were all wrapped up in the early Auden and the middle Eliot. In fact, some people were surprised to think that John Masefield should be Poet Laureate, when he was no longer actively producing much poetry.

I thought of him, then, as the writer of poems and tales of energy, daring, passion, far countries, and the wild sea. I knew, too, that he had led a wandering life when he was young: there were stories about his early training as a seaman, on the last of the sailing ships, and about his being poor in America, working as a bartender somewhere in New York. (He must just have missed serving drinks to O. Henry.) Because of all this, I was surprised, when I met him, to find in him a very gentle, soft-spoken, scholarly, anxious, kindly person, rather more like Gilbert Murray than anyone else. Certainly not like a sea rover or an adventurer—apart from his dark blue suit, like a retired sea captain's, and his odd, pale, distant eyes. The picture on the dust jacket of *So Long To Learn* gives a very good impression of that outward appearance. To it you must add his beautiful soft voice, and his boyish smile, rather surprised at times.

Now, there are puzzles in the lives and characters of most eminent writers; and it seemed to me that there were two puzzles about John Masefield. One was that, although Poet Laureate, he had almost stopped writing poetry. The other was that, although he had led a life which was, at least in part, rough and violent, and although he wrote about rough and violent people, he himself was so quiet, so mild. It is only through reading this book, this part of his autobiography, that I have been able to see my way through both of these puzzles. (Really, though, *So Long To Learn* ought to be read together with other parts of his life story: *New Chum,* which tells of his life on the naval training ship; and *In the Mill,* which describes how he worked as a factory hand in Yonkers.)

The story of his childhood and of his young manhood makes it clear that he was not—as I had supposed—an adventurer who became a writer. I had thought of him as something like Herman Melville, who was a hand on a whaling ship at twenty-two, lived for months among cannibals in the Pacific, and started to write only when his adventures had ended. No, on the contrary, John Masefield was always a writer. He loved poetry from his earliest childhood, and could recite 'John Gilpin' and other poems before he could read. And before he was six, he had read Longfellow's *Hiawatha* and *Evangeline* so often that he knew them partly or wholly by heart. (Children who do not learn to read early and easily are doomed to miss a great deal of pure pleasure all their lives.) And it was not only poetry. He loved stories, thrilling and strange stories. At the age of eight he came across his first Red Indian tale, Mayne Reid's *The War Trail*—which, he says, 'caught him up into the heart of romance.' Apparently, then, John Masefield always wanted to be an author, and he always admired storytellers above most other men. Left to himself, and kept at home, he might have become a gentle writer of fantasies, or perhaps a regional novelist. But his life was interrupted and its course was violently changed: first by his family's sending him off to learn to be a merchant seaman (that killed the faculty of storytelling in him for a time, just as it was developing), and then by some personal trouble, about which we are told little, which made him a homeless poor wanderer in America. (Yet he still loves New York, and calls it 'queen of all romantic cities.') It was only after these diversions were over, when he was in his twenties, poor, and so ill that he was not expected to live, that he was able to recommence—or rather to continue—his real career and become a writer.

Much as he suffered, it was good for him. It taught him many things about men and about the world which he would never have learned, living at home; and it strengthened his character, converting him from a rather too timid and ghost-fearing youngster into a sensitive but courageous and determined man.

Therefore, although his long poems and his stories are full of danger, suffering, and atrocious violence, they are also full of virtue and nobility, which assert themselves above his agony. Indeed, if they have an instantly noticeable weakness, it is that they run to happy endings, almost too pat, almost too complete; but that is not because Masefield wants to please his public: it is because he is fundamentally an optimist, and believes that good always triumphs over evil.

Characteristic is the poem called 'Enslaved': a tale of the sixteenth or seventeenth century, in which a girl is kidnapped by Moroccan pirates and carried off to Safi, to become one of the Khalif's women. Her lover follows her, becoming a slave in order to be near her. He contrives with a friend to make his way into the harem at night, sets her free, and is just stealing out of the city with her when they are captured. The Khalif sentences them all to be flayed alive, and hung on hooks to die, as a penalty and a warning. Then, just before this frightful sentence is to be carried out, the young man's friend speaks his mind, declares to the Khalif that he and his laws are both wrong, and tells how bravely the youth chose to be a galley slave and to bring an awful death upon himself because of the purity and energy of his love. The Khalif listens; admires their courage; sets them all free; and sends them home in safety. You see, Masefield believes that life is not tragedy, but romance and victory.

That, then, is the solution for one of the two problems which struck me about Mr. Masefield—his blend of adventurousness with gentleness. He had always been gentle and thoughtful; but he had been briefly thrust into adventure and violence. The rest of his life he has spent reconciling one extreme with the other.

The second puzzle was more difficult to solve: the puzzle that, although Poet Laureate, he had almost stopped writing poetry, and was indeed little known for his poetic work. Something of that was caused by a change of fashion, by the postwar cult of complex, scholarly, fragmentary poetry like Ezra Pound's. But apart from fashion, I wondered what was the real merit and the real character of Masefield's long poems: so I got hold of them and read them.

Perhaps I, too, had been influenced by the change of fashion, for I didn't care much for them: 'Dauber,' 'The Daffodil Fields,' 'The Everlasting Mercy' . . . they all had fine poetry in them, and they were good stories; but they also had some rather painful letdowns, and the tone varied oddly from prose to poetry, from intense feeling to weak sentiment.

With one exception. One of the long poems, I thought when I first read it, and still think, is one of the best narrative poems in English. It is called 'Reynard the Fox,' and it is a magnificent description of a long, exciting fox hunt, written in a beautiful tempo which begins slowly, with the gathering of the hunters (all described individually), and quickens to a rousing gallop. It is full of sympathy both for the hunters and for the fox himself; and rich with brisk, clear pictures of a handsome English countryside. Chaucer would have been proud of it: a splendid poem.

But the others . . . I turned from them to Mr. Masefield's book again, and there I found the answer. It is this. He thinks of himself not primarily as a poet, but as a storyteller.

For him, poetry is mainly a way of telling a story. And there are other ways—for instance, he tells stories in drama also, and he tells them in prose, as romantic novels.

Having realized this, I turned to those books of his which have always delighted me, and re-read them, too. Still they held up; still they entranced me; still they seemed to me among the finest romances in the language. If you don't know them, let me recommend them warmly. In particular, there are two, about Englishmen wandering in South America, which I must have read forty times. They are called *Sard Harker* (a man's name; 'Sard' means sardonic) and *Odtaa* (o.d.t.a.a., 'one damn thing after another'). Sard Harker was the mate of a first-class ship, and went ashore in a South American port, where he heard, indirectly and accidentally, of a plot to kidnap a girl and maim or murder her brother. The threatened couple lived outside the city. He set out to warn them. By a series of linked accidents, he was stranded, missed his ship, and was carried far into the interior, through one wildly exciting adventure after another, finally crossing a desert and a mountain range, alone among the bears and the eagles, as though in a vision. And when he got back to the seaport city, he was able to find the girl, and to deliver her from a hideous destiny. Throughout this long story Masefield writes both with humorous realism (there is a terribly funny boxing match near the beginning) and with exquisite imagination which makes us see that he *is* a poet, even in prose. This book and the others are in the same line as Stevenson's *Treasure Island*—only better, richer, more adult. When I first read *Sard Harker* and its companions, I could not understand why they gripped me so, and stayed in my mind, since most adventure stories soon slip away. Now I see. It is because they are romances, and romance should be written—whether in verse or in prose—by a poet.

Realistic novels deal with the prose of life. Romances of

travel and adventure deal with its poetry. And it is because of his storytelling that John Masefield has amply earned the right to be called a poet, and to be crowned with laurel.

———

John Masefield, *Collected Poems* (Macmillan, 1935).
In the Mill (Macmillan, 1941).
New Chum (Heinemann, London, 1944).
Odtaa (Macmillan, 1926).
Sard Harker (Macmillan, 1924).
So Long to Learn (Macmillan, 1952).

Enigma with Variations: Donald Tovey

W OULD you believe it possible to remember five musical notes for 20 years? It sounds improbable, doesn't it? And
yet there are five notes which I heard in 1932. I remember
them still, and the evening I heard them, and the man who
played them.

It was a quiet Sunday evening in Oxford, at a piano recital.
The setting: a tall Gothic room with a dais at one end, and
a big fire whispering and smiling in the middle of one wall.
Long wooden tables and benches, at which scores of young
men and women sat in silence, so far as the young are ever
silent; a few had got up into the organ gallery; and some
bold extroverts had perched in the window ledges. The electric lights were out, and there were only candles besides the

firelight. It was rather an occasion, for the pianist was playing in his own college.

He was Sir Donald Tovey, who had been at the college a quarter of a century earlier, with a weird combination of distinction and failure, and had since distinguished himself in many fields. He had dined with his friends among the dons, and had retired with them to chat while the hall filled up.

There was a hush as he came out. I don't remember all the details . . . somehow I think the piano was not up there on the dais as usual, but down in the middle of the hall near the fire . . . Anyhow, Tovey advanced, a tall burly man with white hair and an expression of authority which sat oddly on a curiously youthful face. He sat down and looked at the piano, with that peculiar look which great performers give it when they are not too harried or strained: the look of friendship and mastery, and challenge and fulfillment.

It was one of the finest recitals I have ever heard. In particular, I recall his playing of Beethoven's *Sonata Appassionata, Opus* 57. Tovey's biography tells us that he had been working hard at it twenty-seven years before, and had then doubted whether he could 'make the audience feel it afresh.' Ever since then he had been playing it and thinking about it; doubtless teaching it, too; now, he had grown, he had achieved control as well as passion, both of which are needed for the *Appassionata.* I had never listened to such a performance of the first movement, exciting, and yet *sane*: and his playing of the second movement really took us all into—well, you know the theory of the World-Mind? the idea that, as individuals, we can all think and understand only on a very low plane; but that, through art and religion and philosophy and some other experiences, we can share in the thought of a greater and higher, a universal spirit? So, then, we felt when Tovey played the second movement of the *Appassionata.* And to this day I recall his playing of the five notes which close the first part of the theme. Only these five:

and yet they communicated indescribable things to us; they sang and thought; they moved us and taught us; they helped us to grow.

I never saw Tovey again. Soon after his recital, though, I bought Bach's 48 Preludes and Fugues, with fingering by Harold Samuel and introduction and notes by Donald Tovey. There—as well as meeting the astounding intellect of Johann Sebastian, on which I still feed from year to year (Schumann called the 48 'the musician's daily bread')—I was brought into contact with Tovey's very personal style of writing and explaining. It was uncompromising; and therefore flattering. He assumed that you knew Bach was a supreme genius and that you wanted to meet him; he assumed that you had done (or would do) enough study to bridge the gulf between Bach and you; then he told you the important things to aid you, wittily and shrewdly.

Ever since then I have been reading Tovey's writings at intervals. He really made his name by his contributions to the *Encyclopædia Britannica*: they have been collected separately, and edited by his friend Hubert Foss. But, apart from that, he wrote a great deal—chiefly program notes: a difficult form of exposition to do properly, as you will agree if you have read the bosh which appears on the albums of so many contemporary phonograph records. He ran an orchestra in Edinburgh for over a quarter of a century, and during that time he covered an amazing amount of territory, explaining it as he went. His collected program notes amount to six volumes, and are part of the foundation of a modern musical library. He scarcely ever wrote anything which would not both instruct and amuse. I am particularly devoted to his essays, *The Main Stream of Music.*

Now, who was this man? So I asked myself at intervals. When I lived in Scotland I knew him to be a distinguished musician, who conducted and professed in the slightly distant (and slightly snobbish) city of Edinburgh; but I could never hear him, and his own compositions were never played. He visited Oxford at intervals to lecture or perform, but he was sometimes ill and sometimes distracted, and always elusive. He died in 1940; and he is like some other musicians of the last generation, in that his character and his achievement have not yet been clearly defined. (It is the same, isn't it, with Busoni, and Reger, and Fauré, and Dukas, and Mahler?) But now a useful biography of him has appeared, written by one of his own pupils and friends, Miss Mary Grierson. It is perplexing, but valuable.

Tovey was not Scottish, though his name and career seem to attach him to Scotland. He may have had Scots ancestry, but he was born and brought up in England. (His mother and father were the middle-class eccentrics whom we expect to find as the parents of men of distinction in that period. They paid Donald very little attention, but they were intelligent and charming individuals. His mother once observed at tea time that she needed a new tea cosy, so she picked up a pair of scissors and cut a square out of the velvet curtains. She also knew Dante by heart.)

The boy was obviously meant to be a musician. Neither of his parents was musical; but he was born with it. When he was only four, he went to a baby school with his brother, and sat on the teacher's knee in singing class, while she played the piano. The other children sang the melody. Donald Tovey, aged four, sang the second part, completing the harmony. Miss Weisse, the teacher, could hardly believe her ears; but when the others had gone she tried again. She picked up Schubert's *Heidenröslein,* and played and sang it: the little boy once again sang the second part, although he could not read the music.

Miss Weisse then took over his education, and continued to guide him—some would say dominate him—all through his life. She was a German, with strong will power and sound taste, and she never felt that Donald could be, or should be, left alone: right down to the day of his death. She kept him from going to school; she taught him lots of music, but not much else; she worried when he went to college; she opposed both his marriages and his professorship; she kept a firm grasp on him even when he was sixty; and she outlived him, dying less than a decade ago at the age of ninety-three.

Donald Tovey was a phenomenal pupil. When he was a schoolboy he could read a full orchestral score much as you and I read a newspaper, but remember it better; he was always devoted to the scholarly side of music. There is a story about his taking a train trip alone at the age of twelve, on which he lost his baggage, his hat, and his ticket, but arrived safely with twenty-four miniature scores tucked under his arm. That was like his life. He was always losing what you and I would call the essentials, but he always retained the music.

He went to Balliol College in 1894 with a scholarship, and did extremely well in music. At his final examination, the philosophers thought he should get first-class honors, his papers being 'the best of his time'; but the historians objected that he had omitted most of the required reading. He got third-class honors, and left Oxford with relief and appendicitis.

Then he hit London, appearing with tremendous éclat as a pianist, both solo and in chamber-music groups, and as a composer. He also wrote rather patronizing program notes: after all, he was only twenty-five, and he had a slightly pontifical manner. He was hailed as either a genius or a potential genius; paralleled to Schumann and Brahms; much admired and something disliked. He spent the next fourteen years playing, composing, teaching, and writing . . . but somehow he never became admittedly eminent. He got into quarrels; there was some feeling about his lofty manner; he knew too much; he was a special taste.

In 1914 he was appointed Professor of Music at Edinburgh, and held that post till the end of his life. He was extremely good as a teacher, though erratic and unpredictable; he also organized an orchestra which, in the face of ghastly financial and aesthetic difficulties, carried out a remarkable program of music in its thirty years of life; he wrote an opera, which was produced in 1929 but has seldom been seen and heard since; he wrote a cello concerto for his friend Casals; and he gave hundreds of recitals. For anyone who finds it exhausting to play six Bach preludes and fugues, or a single Beethoven sonata, it is overwhelming to run through Tovey's biography and see what a vast amount of music he wrote, performed, explained, taught, and knew. Naturally he overworked; when I heard him play in 1932 he had been ill, and was aging; he died a few years later, at the age of 64.

Miss Grierson's biography of him is very illuminating, but it does not answer some of the main questions that come to mind. He was a very queer fish, Tovey, but he was a big fish. What kept him from larger recognition? Why do we never hear his compositions? As we read his life we think that he must have been someone like Saint-Saëns, or Dohnanyi—Max Reger comes to mind again, for they both loved counterpoint. What is lacking? Something in our knowledge of him? something in the public to which he addressed himself? something in him?

One answer is that he was discouraged by hostile reviews of his early work. That could be. Rachmaninov was so discouraged, and nearly killed himself: the impulse was transferred into his Second Concerto and *The Isle of the Dead*. But Rachmaninov survived, and went on writing. Then, Tovey had terrific family complications: true, but others have had such complications, and have thriven on them. Was he distracted, perhaps, by his work as a teacher? That may be an answer. It is very hard, harder than most of us imagine, to teach and also to write anything original, without becoming trivial, or neglecting the pupils, and that Tovey would not do.

Or was he crippled by the loving care with which his perpetual teacher surrounded him? Miss Weisse caught him when he was four, and never let go. Worse: she kept hold of him even when she could teach him no more, but merely wished to *guide* him and *control* him and *help* him. She moved into a house next door to him in Edinburgh (he got married the next year), she *worried* about dear Donald, she distrusted his wives and his friends, she thought of him as *my Donald* even when he was an elderly man covered with responsibilities and honors, and far wiser and more creative than she had ever been. Yes, that could be. One of the points about teaching is to leave the pupil alone when he wants to be free and can be free. Miss Weisse did not do for Tovey what Max Perkins did so brilliantly for Thomas Wolfe. Perkins let Wolfe run, and then fly . . .

But possibly we are unjust. Tovey may not have been meant to be a composer. The fact that he gave it up (relatively) shows that he did not feel the same constant urge that was felt by others. As Bach died he was dictating a chorale fugue, *Before Thy Throne I Now Appear;* at the end of Tovey's life he was playing a little and teaching a little. Perhaps he was meant to be a scholar. Not such a high destiny, alas; but still a dedicated career. There are very few good musical critics whom one could parallel to Sainte-Beuve; good teachers of music are still rarer; versatile performers like Tovey are one in a hundred million. It is not an unworthy destiny to be an interpreter of greatness.

Donald Tovey, *Essays in Musical Analysis* (Oxford, 1935-9).
Donald Tovey, *The Main Stream of Music and Other Essays* (collected and introduced by H. Foss, Oxford, 1949).
M. Grierson, *Donald Francis Tovey* (Oxford, 1952).

The Poet and the Modern Stage: Christopher Fry

THERE are three notable English-speaking poets who write verse-drama: T. S. Eliot, W. H. Auden, and Christopher Fry. It is tempting to try to talk about all three of them; but they have really very little in common. They don't form a school. They don't think in the same way. They don't even write in the same patterns and rhythms.

Let us therefore discuss one of them—the one who has written most in the field of poetic drama, and who is more accurately a professional playwright than the others. This is Christopher Fry. Four of his plays have already been produced in New York—the most recent being *Venus Observed,* directed by Sir Laurence Olivier, and acted with considerable skill by Rex Harrison as an elderly wolf and Lilli Palmer as a sleek lamb with a revolver and a Viennese accent. I don't think they always knew what they were saying; but I don't think Christopher Fry always knows what he is writing, or what he wants to say to us. I think he likes to mystify, to joke, to conjure. What does Cardini prove by making a pack of cards appear out of his wrist, and then diminish in size until it becomes invisible?

Christopher Fry is forty-five years old. He comes from the picturesque old seaport of Bristol, out of which John Cabot sailed to discover North America in 1497. I picture him as rather like the cheerful hero of Priestley's fine comic romance, *The Good Companions*: young Inigo Jollifant, who taught a bit, but whose real love was the stage and its gaiety. Fry started very small indeed, in the Repertory Theater of Tunbridge Wells—a little resort town like Asheville.

In 1935 he did the lyrics and music for a revue, which was quite successful. Then he wrote at least three plays for historical and religious pageants. In 1940 he became director of the Oxford Playhouse—a fine institution which has produced a number of notable actors—but then the Army got him. It put him in the Pioneer Corps, where I suppose he rebuilt bombed houses and demolished bridges; but it taught him a lot about ordinary people—which is good for him, since he tends to be a little remote from the common herd.

Soon after the war, in 1946, he wrote a tremendously affected play with a tremendously affected title. Only the audiences were not much affected. This was *A Phoenix Too Frequent*. I like it least of all his work; but certainly it shows that he can handle words and define characters. Critics began to watch Fry, as the gourmets watch a new vintage of Burgundy: he looked as though he might have more body than Auden, more bouquet than Eliot; would he mature in bottle?

Three years later his comedy *The Lady's not for Burning* was produced by John Gielgud, and was a success. It really was both drama and poetry, which is a terribly difficult combination to pull off. Besides this, two recent plays have appeared which are not quite regular dramas and not quite pageants—*A Sleep of Prisoners,* which was played in a Madison Avenue church a year or so ago; and *Thor, with Angels,* written for the festival at Canterbury Cathedral which commemorates the mission of St. Augustine to the pagans of southern England. Recently, in England, a new version of one of his earlier plays was brought out: this is *The Firstborn,* a drama about Moses and the Children of Israel in Egypt. I have not seen or read it, but some say it is his best.

Seven plays, and several pageants. A considerable body of work.

Now, what does it look like?

Two chief subjects seem to interest Fry. One is religion—approached not in the difficult and tragic manner of Eliot, but in a clear, naïve, almost medieval spirit. (Remember that he comes from Bristol, which is full of beautiful medieval churches—or was until the Luftwaffe got to work on it.) The other is—I'm not sure what to call it. Imagination? but that is too vague. Humor? that is too simple. Whimsy is a degraded word. Perhaps we might say *fancy:* the scene of the unexpected, the almost illogical, surrealism without its revolting elements, the same spirit which created *Alice in Wonderland* and *The Hunting of the Snark,* the spirit that dances all through *A Midsummer-Night's Dream* and masquerades in *As You Like It* and haunts the lonely island of *The Tempest.* Quirks of chance, miracles of God, sudden bold conversions of character, daring but incredible deeds, that is what he likes to describe.

The times and places of his plays will also show what he chiefly thinks about: England, southern England, the England of history; the lands of the Bible; and the Greece and Rome of classical antiquity. Nearly all his dramas are historical—but so are many, perhaps most, modern plays. He has a sensitive, though not very deep, feeling for history: roughly, he believes that people are the same in all ages, but that the weaker and stupider are distorted or paralyzed by the social patterns of their own time, while the individuals fight their way through onto something like a permanent level of values.

His style?—

Without an individual style, no poet (still less a poetic dramatist) can hope to make his voice heard. Yet it is one of the hardest things to acquire: it needs long practice, long lonely meditation, and a strong personal character, self-confident, versatile, yet determined. When you are writing verse-drama in English, the temptation to copy Shakespeare is almost irresistible. It entrapped Keats in his *Otho,* and Coleridge, and Tennyson. Fry is not like Shakespeare; although the young Shakespeare would not have disowned some of Fry's best pages. He is a poet in his own right.

The pattern is blank verse, a loose 5-beat iambic line, which will do both for ordinary slangy conversation and for high-flown rhetoric. Here is a prayer to pagan gods, from *Thor, with Angels:*

> Gods, our gods, gods
> Of the long forced-march of our blood's generations
> Dead and living. Goaders, grappling gods,
> Whose iron feet pace on thunder's floor
> Up and down in the hall where chaos groaned
> And bore creation sobbing. Boding gods,
> Who broad in the universe consume our days
> Like food, and crunch us, good and bad,
> Like bones . . .

And here is a comic footman, from *Venus Observed:*

> It's Mrs. Taylor-Snell I'm looking for;
> Oh, that's right, lady, you're here. I have
> A message to give you, they said; prompto . . .

Your old man has got hisself throwed off his horse,
Hunting little rabbits and uvver breeders.
Now, now, lady, you never know,
It may only be a front toof a bit loose.

Above that, the pattern is what you and I would call regular drama: three acts, or one act in three or four scenes; a reasonable number of characters; seldom a chorus; no supernatural figures or massive crowd-effects; economy—but economy without simplicity.

And his dialogue? Perhaps the same phrase would describe it: economy without simplicity. It is brief and brisk, without many long speeches, except in one or two plays at one or two high points; even those long speeches are descriptions or meditations, not big rhetorical declamations soaring to a climax. But the essence of his style is imagery. Scarcely anyone in Fry's plays states a fact or expresses an emotion, without translating it into an image.

For instance, here is a soldier deploring his own bad luck on getting into an uncomfortable situation*:

O history, my private history, why
Was I led here? What stigmatism has got
Into my stars? Why wasn't it my brother?
He has a tacit misunderstanding with everybody
And washes in it. Why wasn't it my mother?
She makes a collection of other people's tears
And dries them all.

Notice the two unexpectedly domestic metaphors, collecting dried tears and washing in discomfort; and the odd word stigmatism (which means 'focusing'). Again, here is a Duke, introducing his son†:

My extension in time: Edgar.

---

* *Phoenix*, p. 15.
† *Venus*, p. 14.

And here is a woman saying that her husband needs rest*:
> Dip him
> In sleep, that blue well where shadows walk
> In water over their heads, and he'll be washed
> Into reason.

Of course, we must not think that all Fry's images are serious or contrived. He is essentially a comic poet, he loves puns, and he loves to play on the sound of words. He will speak of 'original syntax,'† say that a brilliant talker has been 'coruscating on thin ice,'‡ or make a bored man burst out§:

> O tedium, tedium, tedium. The frenzied
> Ceremonial drumming of the humdrum!
> Where in this small-talking world can I find
> A longitude with no platitude?

What use is all this? Is it dramatic, does it help the play? Yes, because it is always lively and unexpected; the essence of drama, one of its essences, is the unforeseen. (As soon as we feel we can tell what is going to happen next, and what the characters will say about it, the drama has died, losing both action and passion. That sounds as though I were beginning to talk like Fry myself.)

Then again, the imagery is valuable because it illuminates new ranges of the mind. In a prose drama, it is hard to make words convey more than their surface meaning; but through poetry, thoughts can acquire several different overtones, and, like the music of an opera, can show the characters more fully and in more complexity, their imagination as well as their emotion, their unconscious thoughts as well as the ideas they realize and speak.

---

* *Thor*, p. 15.
† *Venus*, p. 59.
‡ *Venus*, p. 22.
§ *Lady*, p. 63.

But—and here is a sober criticism—but imagery as Fry often uses it tends to be undramatic, because it blurs the differences between his characters. For page after page it is impossible to tell who is speaking to whom. All except the farcical servants and fools talk in the same elegant profusion of metaphors, with what Mrs. Malaprop would call a nice derangement of epitaphs. The result is that his plays often resemble those pictures by Seurat in which people, and trees, and rivers, and walls all dissolve into brightly colored dots; or the paintings of Dufy, where the New York skyline and the Bois de Boulogne and the sea front at Cannes all swerve and swoop and curve and flicker with the same irresponsible gaiety.

Lastly, how about his plots? They are, frankly, naïve. There is a good deal of movement in them, and some conflict, but little or no development of character. They are nearly all built on one or two unexpected twists: sometimes a miracle, sometimes a flight of amiable fancy. The miracles are put on the stage quite boldly. In *Thor, with Angels,* which I think is my favorite, a pagan of the Dark Ages stands with his foot on the neck of a Christian prisoner, raises a cup to his own gods, and cries*:

We'll drink to our restored prosperity:
The sustaining sinews of tremendous Thor:
The unwearying, turbulent, blazing loins of Woden!
We raise our cups and drink, to the power of the gods,
This toast:

'Let us love one another.'
(*His cup falls from his hand. He stands trembling.*)

In *Venus Observed* a girl burns down her lover's observatory to bring him 'down to earth,' and he at once determines to marry her. In *A Phoenix Too Frequent,* a widow who has just lost her husband and is starving to death in his tomb

* *Thor,* p. 14.

falls in love with a passing soldier, and gives him her husband's corpse to replace one he was guarding: it shows you how pleasant a fellow Fry must be, that this old story is not shown as the triumph of woman's lust over fidelity, but as the miracle of life, which has meaning, conquering death, which has none.

Chances and quirks and miracles—these make drama, too, but it is comic drama. Fry is a thoughtful dramatist, but he is not yet a serious dramatist. There is no sign yet that he can write a tragedy. And there is no sign yet that he can write a great comedy, for the great comedians of the world are those who have looked at tragedy, and still continue to laugh. I like him, but I hope he will soon grow up.

C. Fry, *The Boy with a Cart* (1939) ; *A Phoenix Too Frequent* (1946) ; *Thor, with Angels* (1948) ; *The Lady's not for Burning* (1949) ; *Venus Observed* (1949) ; *A Sleep of Prisoners* (1951). I have not seen Derek Stanford's *Christopher Fry, an Appreciation*.

Dickens as a Dramatist

CHARLES DICKENS was a remarkable novelist. He knew an enormous amount about society. He knew much about the human heart; and much more which he never wrote down. He was technically so skillful that occasionally he did tricks just for the sake of showing his skill, or allowed himself licenses because he knew he could get away with them. And, like many creators, he was something more than a player upon one instrument. He could, of course, tell a straightforward story in a straightforward way. But life does not do so. Dickens liked to imitate, even to outdo, life. Therefore, he sometimes told his stories in unusual ways, making them socially as complicated as Proust's novel is psychologically complicated; or he would move bewilderingly back and forth (as in *Bleak House*) between subjective and objective narration. But there is one particular point about his work which marks it out as different from the achievement of most novelists. This is his passion for the drama.

Prose narrative and plays are both fiction. They both represent the adventures and report the speeches of imaginary characters. Prose fiction is more extensive, drama more intensive. A story can contain 200 characters (and some of Dickens' novels contain at least as many, all alive and kicking, all with characteristic habits and special ways of speaking, with peculiar gestures and with unforgettable names); but a drama can scarcely contain more than ten or twelve. A story may take days to read, a normal play is over in three hours. A story can have thirty climaxes, few dramas can afford more than four or five. A story can pause and reflect; drama always acts and moves. The drama, then, and the novel are different ways of reflecting the world through fiction; but sometimes the novel can borrow techniques from the stage.

Now, Dickens himself began as a reporter. Indeed, he remained a journalist for much of his life: editing a newspaper and two magazines, even issuing his novels not in volumes but in serial parts. But soon after his first success he became interested in another field of publicity: the theater. He loved private theatricals, that peculiar Victorian amusement which is almost as dead now as madrigal-singing. He loved the professional stage, on every level from high drama down to circuses and animal acts. He met his Nemesis, the cold young Miss Ellen Ternan, as she was standing in the wings waiting to go on; and finally he himself took to the stage as a combination of author and actor, in the famous series of Readings where he held huge audiences for several hours on end, simply by reciting the greatest scenes from his novels—not as one reads a story but as one acts a drama, with bold mimicry, tremendous passion, and melting pathos. It was a common thing for people at these shows to burst into tears and faint.

In 1952 Mr. Emlyn Williams repeated some of these Readings on the stage. It was a less flamboyant performance. No one screamed, and indeed Mr. Williams did not attempt the most fearful passages, such as the murder of Nancy from *Oliver Twist* (do you remember how brilliantly the producers of the film version implied that, with Sykes' dog whining and scratching madly at the door to escape?). But it was pretty versatile—including a splendid ghost story called 'The Signalman,' in which gesture and tone of voice were absolutely essential, and a droll passage from *Our Mutual Friend,* in which Mr. Williams, twisting his arms high above his head, imitated a gigantic epergne on Mr. Podsnap's table saying to the guests with a solid silver sneer, 'Wouldn't you like to melt me down?'

Thinking over Mr. Williams' performance, I realized more fully than ever before the truth of something said by Edmund Wilson, in a penetrating paragraph of *The Wound and the Bow*: that Dickens conceived many of the most striking parts of his novels in terms of drama. They are best appreciated if thought of in that way. He himself sometimes imagined life to be most affecting and most satisfying when it was dramatic, and he often preferred intense and striking gestures and characters to the steadier and lengthier tempo of daily existence, as experienced by most of us and told by most writers of fiction.

To begin with, Dickens loved describing players, of every kind. *The Old Curiosity Shop* is rather a dreary novel, apart from the fascinating villain Quilp; but it becomes lively as soon as Nell and her grandfather run away—for the first people they meet are Messrs. Codlin and Short, producers and directors of a Punch-and-Judy show. Shortly afterward they run into Mr. Jerry, who has a troupe of extremely funny dancing dogs. There is a wonderful scene where he feeds them one after the other, while the oldest, in disgrace, goes without his supper and sets off the meal by turning a barrel-organ.

> When any of his fellows got an unusually large piece of fat, he accompanied the music with a short howl, but he immediately checked it on his master looking round, and applied himself with increased diligence to the Old Hundredth [Psalm].

Thereafter Nell rises still higher, and becomes the mainstay of Mrs. Jarley's Wax-Work, 'the delight of the Nobility and Gentry.' In other stories we remember the wonderful company of strolling players led by Mr. Crummles, and the dwarf in 'Mr. Chops,' with his pathetic signature-speech:

> The little man will now go three times around the room, and then retire.

These are players: professionals. But Dickens also loved describing people in the ordinary world who were playing a part. He was (like Shakespeare) haunted by the theme of hypocrisy, and some of his biggest moments describe the unmasking of such men, or actors. There is a short thriller called 'Hunted Down,' written ostensibly by that cool and prosaic person, the manager of a life-insurance office, which introduces a man

> exceedingly well dressed in black, with hair which was elaborately brushed and oiled, and parted straight up the middle. He had an agreeable smile . . . I conceived a very great aversion to that man the moment I saw him.

The man in black turns out to be a skillful murderer, and when he *is* hunted down,

> a singular change took place in his figure, as if it collapsed within his clothes, and they became ill-shapen and ill-fitting.

You see, his impersonation has failed, and his disguise vanishes.

So also Uriah Heep at the end of *David Copperfield* is denounced, and immediately drops the pretense of being 'umble: he snarls,

> Copperfield, I have always hated you.

Is this like Proust, where everyone keeps turning into something else? No, for there they all change, and it is not possible to say that any one character really *is* X and *pretends* to be Y. Both the last pretense and the next pretense are equally part of their essence, and are distinguished only by time and circumstance. In Proust all the characters are made, not by will power and strategy within, but from without, molded by Time and Society, those two relentless pressures. Dickens could not see things so subtly as that, and he himself acted a part throughout the later years of his life, upholding the domestic virtues and yet living with a mistress, wondering which was the real character and which the player, but sure that one was black, the other white.

Then again, we know how much Dickens and his characters love scenes: terrific crises in which all the suspense of months or years comes to a head in fifteen minutes, drastic decisions are taken, and violent alterations of the balance of power take place. In life itself (if we are to judge by the practice of most novelists) things move more slowly, and there is no single point of crisis, but rather a successive group of tensions. But Dickens' characters, like those of the stage, often remain silent for a long time, and then utter all their emotions so violently that nothing is left to say, and we expect only a quick curtain and thunderous applause.

There is a splendid case of this at the end of *Dombey and Son,* when Edith Dombey confronts the sinister smiling Mr. Carker, who believes she has come to be his mistress but learns she has merely used him in order to disgrace her husband and betray himself. It looks rather like the second act of *La Tosca,* the handsome dark-haired woman with the dagger confronting the suave villain.

> 'You have been betrayed, as all betrayers are. I saw my husband in the street tonight.'
> 'Strumpet, it's false!'
> At the moment, the bell rang loudly in the hall.

Another of these big scenes occurs at the end of *Little Dorrit,* where Mr. Pancks gathers the entire population of a slum, Bleeding Heart Yard, to hear him expose the bloodsucking landlord who has always posed as a philanthropist and finishes by cutting off his long, flowing hair and reducing him to a ludicrous booby.

As well as scenes, Dickens loves big speeches, where we can almost see the spotlights falling on the speakers. Sometimes the speeches are delivered outright, accompanied by exclamations from the audience, like Antony's speech in *Julius Caesar;* sometimes they are disgusted, but were obviously conceived for the stage. Thus, at the end of *A Tale of Two Cities,* Sydney Carton is guillotined. No one was allowed to make speeches on the guillotine; and anyhow no one would have understood him in English; so Dickens closes by saying, 'If he had given any utterance to his thoughts, they would have been these...'

and then a page of rhetoric, ending with the famous curtain lines:

> It is a far, far better thing that I do, than I have ever done; it is a far, far better rest that I go to than I have ever known.

And in the denunciation of Heep in *David Copperfield*, Mr. Micawber reads a letter of accusation; but the letter is really a speech, beginning with a splendid exordium about himself:

> The victim, from my cradle, of pecuniary liabilities to which I have been unable to respond, I have ever been the sport and toy of debasing circumstances. Ignominy, Want, Despair, and Madness, have, collectively or separately, been the attendants of my career.

Lovers of Dickens will remember also how many of his best chapters, even without rhetoric, evoke the movements of actors: such as the comic garden scene in *Pickwick*, in which the Fat Boy addresses the deaf old Lady:

> I wants to make your flesh creep—

and tells her about Mr. Tupman's affair with the spinster aunt . . . overheard by the sinister Mr. Jingle.

Or, in *Martin Chuzzlewit*, Jonas, when planning the murder of Montague and putting on his disguise, reminds us inevitably of the elaborate silent 'business' with which actors like Irving used to hold audiences breathless.

The most terrifying of all such passages is in *Bleak House*, where two men are waiting to get some vital papers from the ragman, Krook. His room is below. Their appointment is at midnight. They wait for slow hours. The air is thick. The candle gutters heavily. A foul smell haunts them. Gross smuts hang in the atmosphere, befouling their very clothes. When they open the window, a stagnant sickening oil clings to their fingers. The smell increases constantly, and their horror grows with it, until at last when they go downstairs they are prepared for anything, almost anything—except the worst, the awful discovery that the drunken old ragman has been slowly smoldering to death in the fumes of his own liquor, dying in a sort of hell upon earth, the hell of spontaneous combustion.

Yes, Dickens was a dramatist. Although he never touched the heights of tragedy, he knew a great deal about comedy, and about the farce and the thriller; and that is enough for most of us. Already some spanking films have been made out of *David Copperfield, A Tale of Two Cities, Great Expectations, Oliver Twist,* and *A Christmas Carol.* I hope we shall see more. Emlyn Williams has made an entire evening's dramatic reading out of *Bleak House;* and I should give a good deal to see the burning of Newgate Prison, in *Barnaby Rudge,* or the immortal courtroom of Mr. Justice Stareleigh, where Mr. Sam Weller, when cross-examined by the lawyer opposing his master, is asked: 'You saw nothing of this. Have you a pair of eyes?' and replies, 'Yes, I have a pair of eyes, and that's just it. If they wos a pair o' patent double million magnifyin' gas microscopes of hextra power, p'raps I might be able to see through a flight o' stairs . . . but bein' only eyes, my wision's limited.'

Mr. Eliot

How unpleasant to meet Mr. Eliot!
With his features of clerical cut,
And his brow so grim
And his mouth so prim
And his conversation, so nicely
Restricted to What Precisely
And If and Perhaps and But.
How unpleasant to meet Mr. Eliot! . . . *

So says T. S. Eliot himself, in a sweet-and-sour parody of
Edward Lear, the eccentric, aesthete, and humorist of a

---

* This and the other quotations in this piece are from *Collected Poems
1909-1935*, by T. S. Eliot, copyright 1936 by Harcourt, Brace and
Company.

century ago. It is a funny poem—one of a series called *Five-Finger Exercises,* which are full of parodic allusions to Shakespeare and Keats and Tennyson and Lewis Carroll and Sherlock Holmes and who knows what else?

> How unpleasant to meet Mr. Eliot!
> With his features of clerical cut
> And his brow so grim . . .

However, it is not true. I have never met him myself. I have been in the same room, at least twice, with a host who wanted to introduce me to him; but someone always came up and shook Mr. Eliot's hand and said, 'You know I *loved* your play, the one about the cocktail party,' and he smiled politely and said he was glad. My wife met him later, though, and says he was quite charming. He is a tall, slender man, sometimes bent into the shape of a question mark. He looks like a senior British civil servant; or an eminent surgeon visiting a convalescent patient; or a retired diplomat. . . . He is at the other extreme from the professional romantic, like Walt Whitman with his flying beard, or Carl Sandburg with his healthy open face and boyish hair, the Scandinavian troubadour . . . I suppose Mr. Eliot is now between sixty and seventy; but he looks younger; about fifty; no heavy wrinkles, no superfluous flesh, even his stoop apparently due to politeness rather than fatigue—although that may be a good disguise, and perhaps he really is very weary.

He is a puzzle. He is a strong character: a powerful personality. He must be. Most literary-minded people of my age have been thinking about him (off and on) for a quarter of a century. And yet he has produced this impact *not* by self-advertisement and frequent public appearances; he is rather retiring, both in America and in Britain, and rarely makes speeches or gives lectures; *nor* by writing a great deal, for his entire works could be printed in three or four volumes, and he seldom contributes to magazines or anthologies. No; no. He is a reticent man. He is an enigmatic poet; he wishes to remain a mystery.

Recently Mr. Eliot's collected poems and plays have been published by Harcourt, Brace in a single volume. The book is already a classic. All over the United States, and in Britain and France and Germany and Italy and Japan and elsewhere, students are working over these cryptic and fragmentary poems, writing essays on them, producing technical and sociological interpretations of them, imitating them in their own compositions, and inevitably converting a living man into a myth. But he and his works are still a puzzle. Nobody fully knows what Mr. Eliot's poetry means, except Eliot himself. And, oddly enough, that is part of its power. That is part of the guarantee that it will last. Long after we are dead, people will be arguing about the meaning of Eliot's poems, music will be composed and pictures will be painted and more verse will be written, under the inspiration of a few score pages of poetry by Thomas Stearns Eliot, born in St. Louis, Missouri, educated at Harvard and Oxford, naturalized a British subject, self-described as a royalist, an Anglo-Catholic, and a classicist.

It is a surprisingly small body of work to be so powerful. Just over half the volume is a group of plays, *The Cocktail Party, The Family Reunion,* and *Murder in the Cathedral.* The total of Eliot's serious non-dramatic poetry comes to about 150 pages. 150 pages, for a life's work.

That situates him at once with the mystics, the difficult poets, who have spent many years approaching some truth almost too great for understanding, and trying to say something of what they saw. Such have been St. John of the Cross in Spain; and Hölderlin in Germany; and Henry Vaughan and Donne in England; and Mallarmé and Valéry in France; and, in this country, perhaps Poe. These people had a certain experience of life which they found so complex, so dangerous and alarming, so much profounder than normal thought and living, that they *could not* communicate it in ordinary speech —not even in ordinary poetic speech . . . only in poetry which was deliberately fragmentary and inadequate and symbolic: in just the same way as language itself, compared with the full richness of certain great experiences, is fragmentary, inadequate, and symbolic. (That is why Dante is such a superb writer. He was one of the very few men in the world's history who have had such a vision and have been able to communicate it as a coherent whole. The effort of doing so, the suffering it cost him, are still visible in the portraits of his strong but tormented face. Most others cannot even think of making a complete exposition of such experiences. So all Eliot's poems about this central adventure are indirect, symbolic, incomplete.)

Now, it is hard to understand why a man should spend much of his life on writing, and publishing, and re-publishing a relatively small collection of poems which do not tell the whole truth about the world clearly and single-mindedly. Say the truth, or keep silent; do not confuse us with puzzles. Why trouble to write and print what is only partly intelligible— what is not *meant* to be fully intelligible?

Let us see how it looks. Much of it is in foreign languages; much of it is quotations lifted from other poets, from the Bible and the Prayer Book; much of it is in broken phrases, which do not form complete sentences and paragraphs. It is as though we overheard a musician not playing, but picking over a piano, trying a new harmony here, recalling a favorite phrase there, passing on to something else, but seldom playing continuously for an entire movement.

Blown hair is sweet, brown hair over the mouth blown,
Lilac and brown hair;
Distraction, music of the flute, stops and steps of the
    mind over the third stair,
Fading, fading; strength beyond hope and despair
Climbing the third stair.

There we cannot follow the thought because the utterance is
not coherent. But elsewhere Eliot speaks continuously, and
here we can hardly believe what he says:

A woman drew her long black hair out tight
And fiddled whisper music on those strings
And bats with baby faces in the violet light
Whistled, and beat their wings
And crawled head downward down a blackened wall
And upside down in air were towers
Tolling reminiscent bells, that kept the hours
And voices singing out of empty cisterns and exhausted
    wells.

These are coherent words, but illogical. They are descriptions
of dreams, and suffering, and madness, translated into something beautiful. (You know, many people who like poetry
and art are led to think that poets and artists ought to describe only beautiful things. They believe that a beautiful
poem can *only* be a poem which describes some attractive
experience, that a good picture can *only* be a picture of something which would be attractive to look at in real life. This
is not true, and neither is the reverse true. There are some
eminent artists—their leaders are the great tragedians—who
have been able to make fine poetry, art, and music out of
misery, squalor, and wretchedness. But sometimes it takes
centuries before the public realizes this. I am certain that the
early Christian artists would not have ventured to present to

their public, as a work of art, a painting or a sculpture of the dead Jesus being lifted off the cross on which he had died; but at the highest points of medieval and Renaissance art, the Descent from the Cross was one of the noblest subjects that an artist could choose.)

So, then, Mr. Eliot's poetry is either incoherent or phantasmagorial; and it is an attempt to describe spiritual effort, and agony, and insanity. Is it unique therefore? or unique in our time? No, far from it. Apparently he is saying what other artists have been saying, often incoherently and fantastically, throughout his lifetime. You remember the pale, meager clowns and paupers of Picasso's 'blue period'; and the wildly distorted, yet powerfully memorable, human bodies and animals of his Civil War picture, *Guernica* (even one of the fragmentary heads in it was a classical profile, as it would be in a similar poem by Eliot). You recall the strange roughness of Prokofieff, his irregular rhythms and his moody wandering over the whole range of musical sound; his deliberate difficulty. You will perhaps think also of the mystical obscurity of Vaughan Williams' Sixth Symphony, and of the drifting harmonies of Benjamin Britten, shrill and faint, making, as Eliot himself says,

Out of the sea of sound the life of music . . .

You remember also how Pavel Tchelitchev in his paintings dissects a woman's head, so that you can still see the deep thoughtful eyes and the handsome profile and the curling hair, but also look through to the somber eternal skull within.

I know it is unfashionable to admire Salvador Dali, but I think he is a remarkable painter, and certainly he is sensitive to spiritual currents. Some years ago he was terrified and overpowered by the conception of the atomic bomb. He saw it as the final dissolution of our material universe; and it drove him to meditate upon spiritual structures which are less easily dissolved. Therefore, for the last six or seven years he has been painting pictures which show human and divine figures rushing upward into the air and almost flying into pieces, surrounded by buildings, rocks, and other objects which are flying into pieces; or else floating in mid-air as though suspended by divine power in the moment of an atomic explosion. Perhaps the antithesis is crude: God and the atomic bomb; or more probably I have stated it crudely; but surely the conflict between fragmentation and incoherence on one hand, and stability and poise on the other, is what we experience in Eliot's poems.

Well, then, it is as part of that general movement of thought and emotion that Eliot wrote poems which began by being fragmentary and have very slowly become more complete and balanced, even though they are still cryptic. Evidently it is because he found that his world was broken into fragments—into separate meanings all disconnected or in conflict. He first had to state this spiritual disaster in some form which would be connected, even though it was only a collection of fragments, ruins propped up; then he had to think his way through to a new unity; and to state that new unity in poetry. His *Four Quartets* look like the record of the final achievement: that is why the last of them, 'Little Gidding,' contains a long episode closely resembling Dante, and ends with an image related to Dante's vision of God.

Now, is it worth penetrating any further? Is it worth asking what the explosion was? what was the initial disaster which blew Mr. Eliot's life into the fragments he has ever since been reassembling? Would it be an invasion of privacy to do so? No, surely not, provided we use only the poems, which Mr. Eliot himself has so often republished and therefore wishes to be public knowledge . . . And yet, as soon as we look closely into the matter, we find ourselves embarrassed. The end is God. But the beginning is apparently sex, and some torments arising out of it. From the first part of Mr. Eliot's life, from his twenties, we have some well-organized little satiric poems about the contrast between Europe and New England, about the inadequacy of the middle-class soul. But then, in *The Waste Land,* and perhaps beginning a little earlier, we see a new experience: an experience of *guilt,* involving terrible weakness and inadequacy, blindness and powerlessness, and a life burned away into premature age and lifelong repentance. So his poems seem to say. Some catastrophe, whose cause and course can be guessed, but only guessed . . .

We are not intended to know more. But we are meant to see the work of Eliot's mind gradually remaking itself: a negative and largely pagan soul building itself into a sincere and Christian and self-forgetting soul: a heap of ruins reconstructing itself into a shrine. Others in our lifetime have gone through this, or partly through it. It seems to have happened to Aldous Huxley and to Georges Rouault; we know that it happened to C. S. Lewis; outside Christianity, something like it happened to Paul Valéry and Thomas Mann; there are others, like Koestler and Orwell, who endured the initial disintegration and then were never able to reconstruct their fragments except on an improvised and unsatisfying plan.

If this is true, then we ought to think less of Eliot's poems and more of his plays. They are his largest coherent works. They are problems, which contain solutions. They are positive, solid creations. No doubt they are still oblique approaches to the question of guilt, sin, damnation, self-damnation; but they are more consistent and successful approaches: they present a world which is ultimately sane and manageable, even through martyrdom. So with John Donne: his poems are best understood as the prelude to the wisdom of his meditations and sermons. Mr. Eliot's poems, for all their beauty, are only the prelude to his plays, and to the wisdom of his later life. I hope that when his next volume appears it will establish him as a poetic, as a spiritual playwright: for writing plays—which must be filled with sympathy for many different characters—is one of the best ways for such a sufferer to recreate his world.

——————

T. S. Eliot, *The Complete Poems and Plays* (Harcourt, Brace and Co., New York, 1952).

The Autobiography of Shakespeare

———————

LET us look for a little at Shakespeare's Sonnets. We all know the opening lines of some of them:

> When to the sessions of sweet silent thought
> I summon up remembrance of things past . . .

or this:

> Like as the waves make towards the pebbled shore,
> So do our minutes hasten to their end . . .

or this, the best-known of all:

> Let me not to the marriage of true minds
> Admit impediments. Love is not love
> Which alters when it alteration finds,
> Or bends with the remover to remove:
> O, no! it is an ever-fixèd mark
> That looks on tempests and is never shaken . . .

. . . Yes, we all know *some* of Shakespeare's Sonnets. You remember the story about the old lady who was taken to see *Hamlet* for the first time. After it was over, she said she didn't like it much: the play was good enough as a play, but it was too full of quotations. Everything Shakespeare wrote (even the terrible plays like *Cymbeline* and *The Winter's Tale*) is full of quotations; and there are many in the Sonnets. But although we remember these, very few of us know the Sonnets as a whole, and very very few of us love them. They are not often sold as specially printed gift volumes. Young men seldom buy them and carry them about. When I was eighteen and went for long solitary midnight walks, I had *A Shropshire Lad* in one pocket and *Omar Khayyam* in the other; but it never crossed my mind to carry the Sonnets of Shakespeare. (*Venus and Adonis*, perhaps; but not the Sonnets.) Even critics who write books on the Bard usually play down the Sonnets, discuss them only in the by-going, quote from them less often than from his other works. And yet there are twenty-one pages of them (the same length as *A Midsummer-Night's Dream*); and they contain some of Shakespeare's autobiography, his passions, his weaknesses, the sound of his voice.

But they are difficult to read, and difficult to admire. We cannot follow them closely, we cannot fully understand even the publisher's inscription which opens them, and half the time we can scarcely tell what Shakespeare is talking about.

That is the chief reason why they are so hard to read and enjoy. They are fascinating, but they are enigmatic. In 150 sonnets, all almost exactly the same size and shape, Shakespeare covers more ground than many a modern novel. Dimly, cryptically, he describes . . . not a plot, but a succession of complex situations, terribly hard to understand and yet deeply moving.

They start off unexpectedly enough, with Shakespeare's love for a young man. It is an idealizing love: for, as the Sonnets open, Shakespeare is urging his friend to settle down, get married, and have children. Nevertheless, he talks in terms of passionate admiration, praising the youth's looks, and longing to see him and be near him. Who was the young man? Shakespeare could easily have told us; but he did not mean us to know.

Then there are some peculiar poems about a rival poet—someone (says Shakespeare) of far more talent than he, someone who addresses poems to the same youth, and, by attracting his interest, strikes Shakespeare's own poetry dead. This is very odd, isn't it? Did Shakespeare really think that any other poet was more gifted than himself? If so, when? And who was the other, the ship

> Of tall building and of goodly pride?

Spenser? or Marlowe, whom Shakespeare used to parody in his plays? or Chapman, who was working on a translation of Homer? It sounds like Marlowe . . . but we are not meant to know.

And then, a little later, comes in a woman: a dark woman, the unfashionable color in an England which has always preferred blondes. She had black eyebrows, and 'mourning eyes.' And she was dark also in mind and heart. Shakespeare says he did not especially admire her looks and could not idealize them.

> My mistress' eyes are nothing like the sun;
> Coral is far more red than her lips' red.

And very soon he knew that she was treacherous, a liar, proud, and cruel; still, she had a magical, a haunting power over him, to drive him nearly mad:

O! from what power hast thou this powerful might,
With insufficiency my heart to sway?

Who was she? Perhaps she was Queen Elizabeth's maid of
honor, Mary Fitton. (There is a fine portrait of Mary Fitton
in Carrol Camden's *The Elizabethan Woman*; and she really
looks bewitching.) Anyhow, she not only dominated Shakespeare, but apparently enchanted the youth whom Shakespeare had admired. Once friends, the two became rivals—or
fellow-victims.

And there the Sonnets stop—with no conclusion, and no
resolution, not even a crisis. The last important poem is a
shout of bitter self-reproach in which Shakespeare calls himself a liar and perjurer. Then there are two saccharine sonnets
about Cupid's losing his little arrows: so that the collection
ends not with a pang but a simper. True to life; but unsatisfactory as art. The Sonnets have the fascination of an autobiography, without its clarity. It is like reading an important
document in a cave by the light of matches which keep blow-
ing out.

And then some of us are a little disgusted by their tone.
It is mawkish. It is gushing. It is sentimental. In his plays,
Shakespeare is always in control. His heroes rant madly some-
times, or make silly jokes; but he remains in command.
Therefore it is a shock to see him in the Sonnets, talking more
foolishly than his most affected hero. Instead of sounding like
Hamlet, or even like Romeo, he too often sounds like Mal-
volio.

Like all Shakespeare's work, the Sonnets are full of splendid
lines. True. But here is another snag. Unlike most of his
work, they are also full of bad lines. Some of them are atrocious. They are so bad that they are embarrassing, and several
scholars have suggested that inferior poets must have written

them and foisted them in. Shakespeare could never resist a pun, and went on punning all his life, with reasonable success; but the puns in the Sonnets are really punishing. For instance, his first name to his friends was Will: so he writes stuff like this:

> Whoever hath her wish, thou hast thy Will,
> And Will to boot, and Will in overplus.

It is even worse when he recalls how he first met his friend:

> To me, fair friend, you never can be old,
> For as you were when first your eye I eyed,
> Such seems your beauty still.

Elsewhere, he can make even such silly talk into poetry. When Rosalind babbles like that, it is delightful. In Shakespeare's own voice, it is painful.

But of course, we don't know *when* he wrote the Sonnets, do we? We think of him as the magnificent poet of *Antony and Cleopatra*, the deep psychologist of *Hamlet*, the grim cynic of *Coriolanus*. That he became. But after you read the Sonnets two or three times, you find it hard not to believe that, when he wrote them, he had never composed a single play. Leaf through his dramas. Read the gay, easy rhetoric of *King John*, the musical fireworks of *A Midsummer-Night's Dream*. Then turn back to the Sonnets—and at once you see that they are the work of an amateur, a beginner. Often they repeat the same idea two or three times, as though his fancy were pouring out variations which his taste could not distinguish nor his art suffice to concentrate. They rhyme neatly, they scan, they balance; but they constantly fall into that dismal region lying between poetry and prose, where we are neither soaring on wings nor walking along firm earth, but jolting painfully along on a nervous and ill-trained horse. Here is the end of a sonnet to Time:

> This I do vow, and this shall ever be;
> I will be true, despite thy scythe and thee.

Here is the close of a poem to his friend:

> Look what is best, that best I wish in thee:
> This wish I have; then ten times happy me!

You will ask: how could a gifted poet write such stuff, not once only, but again and again? No one knows the whole answer, because no one fully understands Shakespeare; and, because he was a very complicated character, the answer must be extremely complex. But certainly one part of the answer is the obvious one: when he wrote the Sonnets, he was *young, very young*. He possessed his talents, but he was not sure of them and had scarcely learned how to use them. He had written two narrative poems, acted a little, perhaps; collaborated on a play, possibly; but never yet attempted to create a universe out of his own imagination.

Not long ago, the sharpest detective in English literary history wrote an essay on this problem. Mr. Leslie Hotson, in *Shakespeare's Sonnets Dated,* gives good reason for believing that they came out in 1589, when Shakespeare was only twenty-five. If this is correct, we can easily understand why the Sonnets embarrass us. They are like a very young man's love, passionate but awkward. And as literature, they are timid and conventional—whereas the mature Shakespeare was to become bold and powerful.

Once we are sure of this, we can return, and read the Sonnets with far more enjoyment. Even the silliest things in them are now seen to be not the blunders of a fine poet, but the first sketches for the masterpieces that were later to come from the same mind. For instance, remember the pun on the word *I*? It reappears four or five years later in the mouth of a loving girl:

Hath Romeo slain himself? Say thou but AYE,
And that bare vowel I shall poison more
Than the death-darting EYE of cockatrice:
I am not I, if there be such an AYE . . .

So, also, the bitter experiences through which the young
Shakespeare was then living were later to be concentrated
and reheated until they became the incandescent lava of
Othello's passion, the bitter fumes of Timon's world-hatred.
In the finest of the Sonnets, we can see him practicing the
inimitable eloquence of his mature life, the silver tongue fed
by a golden thought:

They that have power to hurt and will do none,
That do not do the thing they most do show,
Who, moving others, are themselves as stone,
Unmovèd, cold, and to temptation slow;
They rightly do inherit heaven's graces,
And husband nature's riches from expense;
They are the lords and owners of their faces,
Others but stewards of their excellence.

The summer's flower is to the summer sweet,
Though to itself it only live and die,
But if that flower with base infection meet,
The basest weed outbraves his dignity;
For sweetest things turn sourest by their deeds;
Lilies that fester smell far worse than weeds.

Such lines could well be spoken in the greatest of his plays.
And so, as we look at the Sonnets, and see them for what
they are—a preparation for something better—we can understand the comparative failure of much modern poetry. The
Sonnets are really a description of Shakespeare's private
world: that is the chief reason why they are interesting; and

it is also the reason why they are inferior to the rest of his work. So many modern poets prefer to inhabit their own narrow universe, and cannot or will not enlarge it. But, after the Sonnets, Shakespeare spoke no more in his own voice. It was too limited. You remember how Juliet says of Romeo:

> When he shall die,
> Take him and cut him out in little stars.

In the same way, Shakespeare cut himself out into hundreds of men and women. Through his plays, he made his own distracted and eloquent heart into a huge and busy and delightful world, which we still are honored to inhabit.

———

L. Hotson, *Shakespeare's Sonnets Dated* (Oxford, 1949).

The Old Gentleman

THE old gentleman was riding round his land. He had retired several years ago, after a busy career; but farming was what he liked, and he knew that the best way to keep farms prosperous was to supervise them in person. So, although he was approaching 70, he rode round his property for four or five hours, several days each week. It was not easy for him, but it was not difficult either. He never thought whether a thing was easy or difficult. If it ought to be done, it would be done. Besides, he had always been strong. Although his hair was white and his eyes were dimming, he stood a good six feet and weighed 210 pounds. He rose at four every morning. It was December now, Christmas was approaching, snow was in the air, frost and snow on the ground. This month he had been away from home on a toilsome but necessary trip; and in the hard weather he had been able to ride over his farms very seldom. Still, he liked to see them whenever he could. The land was quiet; yet a deal of work remained to be done.

There was much on the old gentleman's mind. His son had come home from college in some kind of disturbance and uneasiness, unwilling to go back again. Perhaps he should be sent elsewhere—to Harvard, or William and Mary? Perhaps he should have a private tutor? . . . Meanwhile, in order to teach him habits of quiet and undistracted industry, 'I can [the old gentleman wrote to a friend], and I believe I do, keep him in his room a certain portion of the twenty-four hours.' But even so, nothing would substitute for the boy's own will power, which was apparently defective. The grandchildren, too, were sometimes sick, because they were spoiled. Not by their grandmother, but by their mother. The old gentleman's wife never spoiled anyone: indeed, she wrote to Fanny to warn her, saying emphatically, 'I am sure there is nothing so pernisious as over charging the stomack of a child.'

He thought hard and long about the state of the nation. Although he had retired from politics, he was often consulted, and he kept closely in touch. One advantage of retirement was that it gave him time to think over general principles. Never an optimist, he could usually see important dangers some time before they appeared to others. This December, as he rode over the stiff clods under the pale sky, he was thinking over two constant threats to his country. One was the danger of disputes between the separate States and the central government. (Congress had just passed a law designed to combat sedition, and two of the States had immediately denounced it as unconstitutional. This could lead only to disaster.) The other problem was that respectable men were not entering public life. They seemed to prefer to pursue riches, to seek their private happiness, as though such a thing were possible if the nation itself declined. The old gentleman decided to write to Mr. Henry, whom he considered a sound man, and urge him to re-enter politics: he would surely be elected if he would consent to stand; and then, with his experience, he could do much to bridge the gap between the federal government and the States.

The old gentleman stopped his horse. With that large, cool, comprehensive gaze which every visitor always remembered, he looked round the land. It was doing better. Five years ago his farms had been almost ruined by neglect and greed. During his long absence the foremen had cropped them too hard and omitted to cultivate and fertilize, looking for quick and easy profits. Still, even before retiring, he had set about restoring the ground to health and vigor: first, by feeding the soil as much as possible, all year round; second by 'a judicious succession of crops'; and third, most important of all, by careful regularity and constant application. As he put it in a letter, 'To establish good rules, and a regular system, is the life and the soul of every kind of business.' Now the land was improving every year. It was always a mistake to expect rapid returns. To build up a nation and to make a farm out of the wilderness, both needed long, steady, thoughtful, determined application; both were the work of the will.

Long ago, when he was only a boy, he had copied out a set of rules to help in forming his manners and his character —in the same careful way as he would lay out a new estate or survey a recently purchased tract of land. The last of the rules he still remembered. *Keep alive in your breast that little spark of celestial fire called Conscience.* Some of the philosophers said that the spark from heaven was reason, the power of the intellect, which we share with God. The old gentleman did not quarrel with them, but he did not believe them. He knew that the divine fire in the spirit was the sense of duty, the lawfulness which orders the whole universe, the power of which a young poet then alive was soon to write

> Thou dost preserve the stars from wrong;
> And the most ancient heavens, through Thee, are fresh
>   and strong.

His mind turned back over his long and busy life. He never dreamed or brooded, but he liked to note things down, to plan them and record them. Now, on this cold December day, he could recall nearly every Christmas he had ever spent: sixty at least. Some were peaceful, some were passed in deadly danger, many in war, some in strange lonely places, some in great assemblies, some in happiness and some in anguish of soul, none in despair.

One of the worst was Christmas Day of twenty-one years before. That was early in the war, a bad time. It snowed four inches on Christmas. His men were out in the open, with no proper quarters. Although he started them on building shelters, an aggressive move by the enemy made them stand to arms and interrupt all other work for nearly a week. And they had no decent uniforms, no warm coats, no strong shoes, no regular supplies, two days without meat, three days without bread, almost a quarter of his entire force unfit for duty. He was receiving no supplies from the government, and he was actually meeting opposition from the locals. They had sent up a protest against keeping the troops in service during the winter. Apparently they thought you could raise an army whenever you needed one—not understanding that this little force was the only permanent barrier between them and foreign domination. He had replied with crushing energy to that protest. In a letter to the President of Congress, he wrote:

I can assure those gentlemen that it is a much easier and less distressing thing to draw remonstrances in a comfortable room by a good fire side than to occupy a cold, bleak hill, and sleep under frost and snow without clothes or blankets. However, although they seem to have little feeling for the naked and distressed soldiers, I feel superabundantly for them, and from my soul I pity those miseries which it is neither in my power to relieve or prevent.

He ended with his well-known, strongly and gracefully written signature, *G. WASHINGTON*.

The year before that, 1776, things had been nearly as bad—the same difficulty about uniforms and supplies. Late in December he wrote earnestly from his camp, 'For godsake hurry with the clothing as nothing will contribute more to facilitate the recruiting service than warm & comfortable clothing to those who engage . . . The Commissary informs me that he cannot prevail on the millers to grind; & that the troops in consequence are like to suffer for want of flour . . . This must be remedied by fair or other means.' However, his chief concern then was not supplies, nor discipline, nor defense, but attack. On Christmas Day, long before dawn, he was crossing the Delaware River at McKonkey's Ferry, with a striking force of over two thousand men. He spent Christmas morning marching to Trenton. Next day he attacked Colonel Rahl and his Hessians. Half of them were sleeping off their Christmas liquor, and nearly all were paralyzed with drowsiness and astonishment. Hungry and hopeful, the Americans burst in on them like wolves among fat cattle. The surprise was complete. The victory, prepared on Christmas Day, was the first real success of the war.

Two winters later at Christmas time, Washington was in

Philadelphia to discuss the plans for next year's campaign with a Congressional committee. People were very civil; they called him the Cincinnatus of America; and some of them made an effort to take the war seriously. But many did not. He would rather have been in winter quarters with his men. A few days before Christmas 1778 he wrote to Mr. Harrison that, as far as he could see, most people were sunk in 'idleness, dissipation, and extravagance . . . Speculation, peculation, and an insatiable thirst for riches seem to have got the better of every other consideration and almost of every order of men.'

Year after year he was in winter quarters at Christmas time, usually in a simple farmhouse, 'neither vast nor commodious,' in command of a starving and bankrupt army. In 1781, after Yorktown, things were a trifle better, and he had dinner with his wife and family at Mr. Morris's in Philadelphia amid general rejoicing. But the following Christmas was the blackest ever. He had thought of asking for leave, to look after his 'long neglected private concerns'; but the army was very close to mutiny, which would have meant the final loss of the war and the probable collapse of the entire nation. It was not only the enlisted men now, it was the officers: they were preparing to make a formal protest to Congress with a list of their grievances; and only the personal influence of Washington himself, only his earnest pleading and his absolute honesty and selflessness, kept the little force in being through that winter.

Yet by Christmas the next year, in 1783, it was all over. Washington said farewell to his officers, and then, on December 23rd, he resigned his commission. His formal utterance still stands, grave as a monument:

> Happy in the confirmation of our Independence and Sovereignty, and pleased with the opportunity afforded

the United States of becoming a respectable nation, I resign, with satisfaction, the appointment I accepted with diffidence: a diffidence in my abilities to accomplish so arduous a task, which, however, was superceded by a confidence in the rectitude of our cause, the support of the supreme power of the Union, and the patronage of Heaven.

So he said. And the President of Congress replied, in terms which, although still balanced and baroque, are more emotional and almost tender:

We join you in commending the interests of our dearest country to the Almighty God, beseeching him to dispose the hearts and minds of its citizens, to improve the opportunity afforded them of becoming a happy and respectable nation. And for you, we address to him our earnest prayers, that a life so beloved may be fostered with all his care; that your days may be happy as they have been illustrious; and that he will finally give you that reward which this world cannot give.

Next day Washington left for Mount Vernon, and spent Christmas 1783 at home in peace.

Some years passed. December was always busy. Washington was on horseback nearly every day, riding round his place, directing the operations which kept the land alive and fed all those who lived on it, ditching, threshing, hog-killing, repairing walls, lifting potatoes, husking corn. And it was a poor December when he did not have at least half a dozen days' hunting, though in that thickly wooded country he often lost his fox and sometimes hounds too. For Christmas after Christmas in the 'eighties, his diary shows him living the life of a peaceful squire, and on the day itself usually entertaining friends and relatives. On Christmas Eve 1788, Mr. Madison stayed with him, and was sent on to Colchester next day in Washington's carriage.

Again a change. Christmas 1789 saw him as the first President of the United States, living in New York, the capital of the Union, and receiving formal calls from diplomats and statesmen. In the forenoon he attended St. Paul's Chapel; in the afternoon Mrs. Washington received visitors, 'not numerous, but respectable'; and next day Washington rode out to take his exercise. (He and Theodore Roosevelt were probably the finest horsemen of all our Presidents; those who knew him best liked to think of him on horseback, the most graceful rider in the country.) But for years thereafter his exercise was cut short and his days were swallowed up in the constant crowding of business. He rarely saw his land and seldom visited his home. His Christmases were formal and public; brilliant, but not warm; not holidays.

But now, after his final retirement, he had time to look back on earlier Christmases. Some of them were very strange. Christmas of 1751 he had spent at sea. His elder brother Lawrence, frail and overworked, sailed to Barbados for a winter cruise, and George accompanied him. On November 3rd, they landed at Bridgetown, and were invited to dine next day with Major Clarke, O.C. British forces. Washington observed gravely to his diary: 'We went,—myself with some reluctance, as the smallpox was in his family.' Less than two weeks later Washington was down with smallpox, which kept him in bed for nearly a month; but he recovered with very few marks. By December 25th he and his brother were sailing back, past the Leeward Islands. As he liked to do all through his life, he noted the weather ('fine, clear and pleasant with moderate sea') and the situation ('latitude 18°30″');

and, with a youthful exuberance which he soon lost, he adds: 'We dined on a fat Irish goose, Beef, &^{ca} &^{ca}, and drank a health to our absent friends.'

Five years later, he was a colonel engaged in one of the wars that helped to make this continent Anglo-Saxon instead of Latin: the war to keep the French, pressing downward along the Ohio from Canada and upward along the Mississippi from New Orleans, from encircling the British colonies in an enclave along the coast and cutting them off forever from the wealth of the plains, the rivers, and the distant, fabulous Pacific. Those two Christmases Washington could recall as a time of profound depression, filled with the things he hated most: anarchic competition and anarchic indiscipline. He commanded a Virginia regiment; and Captain Dagworthy of the Maryland troops at Fort Cumberland would not supply him. He despised drunkenness and slack soldiering; and he would not tolerate the attempts by the liquor trade to batten on his troops and run local elections by handing out free liquor. His enemies beat him temporarily, not by bending his will, but by wrecking his health. Christmas 1757 saw him on leave after a physical collapse which looked very like an attack of consumption, involving hemorrhage, fever, and a certain hollowness of the chest which never quite left him. He bore up as well as he could under the barrage of slander which his enemies poured in upon him, including the foulest of all, that he was accepting graft; but he had been ill for months when he finally broke down. (Years later, when he was appointed Commander-in-Chief, he was offered a regular salary, but refused to accept it. Instead, he asked Congress to pay his expenses; he kept the accounts scrupulously; and he presented them without extras at the end of the war. Slanders are always raised about great men; but this one slander was never leveled at Washington again.)

He looked back beyond that to one of the hardest Christmases in his memory. That was the Christmas of 1753, when he was only 21. Governor Dinwiddie had determined to stop the encirclement of Virginia. The French were building forts on the Ohio, and arresting traders from the British colonies who penetrated that territory. Soon there would be nothing westward except a ring of hostile Indians supported by arrogant French officers. Isolated by land, the colonies could later have been cut off by sea, too, and the seed would have withered almost before it struck firm root.

The governor commissioned young Major Washington to make his way to the French fort, to deliver a letter from him to the French commandant, and to bring back both a reply and an estimate of the situation. He did; but he was very nearly killed. Not by the French. Or not directly. They merely told him that they were absolutely determined to take possession of the Ohio territory, and returned a diplomatic but unsatisfactory reply to the governor's letter. Still, Major Washington had at least the substance of a good intelligence report, for he had inspected the fort and his men had observed how many canoes the French were building. He had only to return. The French, however, endeavored to persuade him to go up and interview the governor of French Canada; and, that failing, set about bribing the Indians in his party with liquor and guns either to leave him altogether or to delay until the worst of the winter, when travel would be impossible for months. But Washington had a good guide; he was friendly with the Indian chief; and he had a tireless will. He set off on the return journey about the third week in December, when snow was already falling heavily mixed with rain. Six days were spent on a river full of ice. The canoes began to give out. The horses foundered. The rest of the party went more and more slowly. Major Washington 'put himself in

Indian walking dress' and pushed on, on foot. On Christmas Day he was making his way toward the Great Beaver Creek. Next day he left the entire party to follow with horses, money, and baggage, and set out alone with the guide, Christopher Gist.

Next day a lone Indian who pretended to know the territory, but who was evidently a French agent, spent some hours leading the two men off their route, and finally shot at the young officer from close range. Gist would have killed him; but Washington would not allow it: they kept him for several hours, and then let him go. Then they pressed on eastward. They had to cross the swollen, ice-jammed Allegheny River. They built a raft; but they could force it only half-way through the roaring current and the hammering ice-blocks. That night they spent freezing on an island in midstream. In the morning, they struggled across on the ice, and pressed on again. In his journal the guide recorded that the major was 'much fatigued.' But still he kept going: eighteen miles a day with a gun and a full pack, over rough territory, threatened by hostile Indians, in mid-December, with snow and rain falling from the sky and lying thick on the ground.

Now, over a period of forty-five years, he looked back on that Christmas. It had been, he remembered, 'as fatiguing a journey as it is possible to conceive'—and still a necessary one. It was the first of his many services to his country, to keep it from being surrounded and strangled from without or poisoned from within. And he reflected that it is not necessary to try to be brave, or clever, or generous, or beloved, or even happy. It is necessary simply to do one's duty. All else flows from that. Without that, all else is useless.

Darkness closed in early in these winter days. It was getting toward Christmas of the year 1798. General Charles Pinckney and his lady were expected for Christmas dinner. The old gentleman finished looking over the land, and turned homeward. He paid no heed to the cold.

———

R. G. Adams (ed.), *Journal of Major George Washington* (Scholars' Facsimiles, New York, 1940).

C. H. Ambler, *George Washington and the West* (Chapel Hill, 1936).

W. S. Baker, *Itinerary of General Washington* (Lippincott, 1892).

W. S. Baker, *Washington after the Revolution* (Lippincott, 1898).

G. W. P. Custis, *Recollections and Private Memoirs of Washington* (ed. B. J. Lossing, Derby & Jackson, New York, 1860).

J. C. Fitzpatrick (ed.), *Diaries of George Washington, 1748-1799* (Houghton Mifflin, 1925).

J. C. Fitzpatrick (ed.), *Writings of George Washington* (U. S. Government Printing Office, 1931-44).

D. S. Freeman, *George Washington* (Scribner, 1948—).

P. L. Haworth, *George Washington, Country Gentleman* (Bobbs Merrill, 1925).

D. M. Larrabee (ed.), *Journal of George Washington* (Allegheny College, 1924).

T. Lear, *Letters and Recollections of George Washington* (Doubleday, Page, 1906).

J. M. Toner (ed.), *Daily Journal of Major George Washington* (Munsell, Albany, 1892).

Places

The West

THE train jogs on persistently, skirting an occasional hill, rumbling through a little valley now and then, but most of the time dead straight and dead level. Chicago is far behind. Town after town follows in a series, all much the same in appearance, and all called PURINA CHOWS. Farm after farm passes, looking pretty prosperous. The big trucks gun their way along the highroad parallel to the train. As night falls, the towns seem to get smaller, and the lights of the farms to shine out more solitarily. All day we have been rolling through the fields where the wheat and the hogs come from; but now the land is getting poorer. As we climb into bed in the sleeper, the last farm lights have disappeared, drowned in darkness and isolation.

And when we wake up next morning, we are in a new

country. No more fields, with long rows of cornstalks. No more tall silos. Even the houses have changed. Instead of being plump and white-and-red like a group of Iowa girls, they are long and thin and dust-colored and casual, like the brown-faced men who stand at the occasional stations (much farther apart now) and watch us quietly. Every so often we pass a big wooden jigsaw of fences and runways, with drinking troughs near by: a loading platform for cattle. This is cow country, and we are in the West.

The land, the air, and the sky change. The air is keener, thinner, with a tang of the mountains. The sky is a paler blue, as though it had been well washed and well dried by mountain rain and wind. The earth is flat no longer. It begins to roll. Away back there in the Heartland, it was country you could walk over or drive through pretty steadily and monotonously. Now it is riding country, and its contours are like the rhythms of a cantering horse. From time to time, like a horse pulled back on his haunches, big rocky bluffs stand apart from the railroad, watching the train. We feel that as soon as we have passed, they may gallop away over the plains. The country gets rougher and lonelier—although not cruel, yet less kind. Man and his works are less important. The occasional highroad and filling station is soon lost; even the line of steel which we leave behind seems to sink away into the prairie like a disused trail. Words like *comfort* and *security*, words like *anxiety* become meaningless, and roll along like the tumbleweed before the wind. And then, quite soon, within a few hours, almost before we have time to appreciate the change in ourselves, the land has changed again; and, as the train rounds a curve, we begin to see the best part of the United States—the tall, dark, princely range, with shoulders clothed in eternal green and heads crowned with cold, blazing white: the Rocky Mountains.

Yes, that is the West: much loved, but still little known. In particular, there are not half enough good books about the West. It is easy to see why. Most authors live in cities, and worry; or in small towns, and think. But if you live out West, you simply live—simply, but fully; you feel it is too good, too rich to describe.

The Westerners themselves seldom try. It is not that they are all taciturn, although some are. Many will talk for hours and hours, as easily as a horse switches his tail. But they don't do straight description or realistic narrative. They tell long incredible stories about people; or engage in long debates about how to do something necessary and difficult, like dehorning. But they will not try to portray a storm in the Big Horns. They will talk about a dance, but they won't compete with Sibelius and describe a night ride toward the sunrise.

Still, there are a few fine books about the West—which deserve all the more respect for their authors' courage in tackling such a tough subject.

To begin with, there are some descriptive works, which take one part of the multifarious western region, explain its physical appearance, tell stories about its past, portray its people and its animals, and try to capture the ethos of the whole area. Such are the books of Erna Fergusson—*Our Southwest* and *New Mexico*. Such is Frank Waters' book about the Colorado River, and his wonderful work on Indian religion and dancing, *Masked Gods*.

Closely allied to these are the books of folklore and history, which are still too few. Any imaginative writer who wanted training might do well to study the history of one range, or one county, or one of the big trails. I remember a fairly good one, with lively illustrations, by R. G. Cleland, called *This Reckless Breed of Men,* about the trappers and fur traders of the Southwest. And one eminent writer has explored the whole field, both physically and historically: we all owe a large debt to Bernard De Voto.

As for fiction—of course there have always been novels about the West, ever since the first Redskin Bit the Dust. Most of them have been constructed on the same simple plan as the country itself, with the Good standing as high as Pike's Peak, the Evil running as deep and dark as the gorge of the Colorado, and the Banality as broad as the King Ranch. Still, the standard has been rising recently. Do you remember A. B. Guthrie's pair of westward-bound stories, *The Big Sky* and *The Way West*? Handsomely written, with a lean spare style which hinted almost as much as it said. Perhaps just a little too sour and negative? Perhaps . . . Mr. Guthrie's Western riders and explorers are silent and lonely men. But he made them silent and lonely because they hated the townspeople and the crowds and the conventions and the smells of civilization. The others, those who pioneered across the mountains into Oregon, loved the family and the togetherness, and were longing to settle down and build; but, according to Mr. Guthrie, the men like Boone Caudill hated most of mankind. Well, perhaps he is right. He knows a great deal more about the West than I do.

Two fine books by H. L. Davis, *Honey in the Horn* and *Winds of Morning,* emphasize the other aspect of the Western character—its cheery, devil-may-care energy, its wild, unbelievable jokes, and its almost meaningless violence. O. Henry —who knew more about America than any single writer up to date—brought this same part of its spirit into several gay short stories, for instance in *The Heart of the West.*

But there is a still harsher side of Western life, which you and I never see: the long tough winters, the cramped quarters, the months of loneliness, the brooding, the hard game between good and evil (or perhaps between humanity and inhumanity) in which the other side seems to hold all the aces, and the Westerner has to bluff hard to stay in. That side comes out memorably in Walter Van Tilburg Clark's books. *The Track of the Cat* begins with a man waking in the dark of a lonely ranch house, to hear his cattle bawling, distantly, through the bitter wind. He knows that a mountain lion is attacking them, and that he has to get out and face it. Clark's *Ox-Bow Incident* was even gloomier; but, like all good Western books, it shows us that the essentials of life are few, and that one of them is courage.

We can get even closer to the West, and to the men who made it, in occasional autobiographies. Sometimes an old rider will dismount, and, having told yarns all his life, will elect to tell them once more to a friendly recorder, who puts them through the press. Elsewhere we have praised *The Memoirs of a Monticello Slave* and *The Letters of Private Wheeler*. I should like to read such books from all over America. I wonder if there are any memoirs by the captains of the New England clipper ships, or by slave traders, or by the people who ran the underground railway which helped to wreck the slave trade? Three or four years ago I came across a delightful autobiography by an old Arizona cowboy, who had for a long time been almost more of an Indian than a white man. It was called *Cow by the Tail*, by Jesse James Benton. When he was 17, he nearly married a Comanche and joined the tribe: she gave him sweet Injun kisses 'under the blanket,' and she danced with him, and finally she showed him her best trick, which was leaping from her horse onto the back of a wild buffalo and riding him for a mile, then stabbing him to death. Taloa she was called. She was pretty, and kind to him; but her tribe once hunted down three white strangers and almost took their scalps. Benton left; still, he remembered Taloa all his life, with her white teeth.

And now I have found another such book, an autobiography called *Pistol Pete*. Its author, Frank Eaton, was born in Hartford, Connecticut—which sounds quiet enough. But his father moved west, in 1867 or so, and settled down to homestead near Lawrence, Kansas. That was troubled country then, and the Civil War was still being fought. Within a year the little boy's father was shot dead in his own house by six men. (Four of them had been among Quantrill's raiders.) In these few minutes, the youngster grew up. He says:

> I fell on [my father's] body screaming. One of the men got off his horse and pulled me away. He kicked me and hit me with his riding-whip. Then he emptied his gun into my father's body and cried, 'Take that, you god-damned Yankee!' Then they galloped away; but *I had seen their faces*. They were the four Campseys and the two Ferbers.

Within a few days, young Frank Eaton had got a gun from a friend of his father's, and was practicing how to make bullets, how to load, how to aim, and how to fire. He learned how to draw, later. By the end of that year, he could shoot a rattlesnake's head off with either hand. He grew up quite normally, helping with the chores, and later riding the range for a neighboring cattleman. But he was certain that, as soon as he was fit to, he was going to kill the men who had murdered his father and ridden away. With this sense of purpose, he did what a boy can sometimes do. He turned play into work and work into play: many hours of the time that ordinary youngsters pass in throwing a baseball or in whittling, he spent in practicing with his guns. When he was sixteen, he found the first of the six men, one of the Campsey brothers. He walked up to Campsey as he sat on his porch at the alert, with a Winchester rifle over his knees, hailed him, saw him raise his rifle, and killed him with two bullets before he could fire. (This was the man who had kicked and whipped the boy over his father's corpse.) By the time he was twenty-one, he had killed all the rest of the gang, or seen them dead.

You might think all this would make him bitter, or slightly crazy, or permanently lawless. On the contrary. He was a law-abiding citizen. For much of the time, in spite of his youth, he was a deputy marshal. He seems to have thought of the entire thing as simply an assertion of the law against lawlessness, an extension of the law to places where it could not formally reach. The rest of his life, after he settled down, is told in a few pages, and interests both him and us less. But the first 250 pages are full of good stories, some grim and some very funny—about that old time which, although old, is not dead either in memory or in ideal.

Shapeless and episodic as they are, such books are in an ancient tradition. They sound like Plutarch's *Sayings of the Spartans* or like the Icelandic sagas. They take us back not merely a few years or decades, but centuries, into a simpler age. That is the kind of life it is, in the West. It would be a shame if it were ever modernized, and spoiled by being converted into an appendage to the cities—a sort of Vacationland. For all its beauty, Yosemite in the summer feels like the Bear Mountain area, with every parking place full, and the smell of gasoline drifting on every breeze. Nature still has her grandeur, but has lost her loneliness and her repose. But fortunately there is enough room out West. Wyoming is lonely. Few people live in Montana; almost nobody lives in Idaho; parts of Utah are still unexplored. The cities where we exist are middle-aged and crowded and jittery. Out there, the plains and the mountains and the life in them are both very old and wise, and very young and strong. To spend some time there, by books or by living, is to shed worries and the accretions of day-by-day activity, and to become your own ancestor.

J. J. Benton, *Cow by the Tail* (Houghton Mifflin, 1943).

B. A. Botkin (ed.), *A Treasury of Western Folklore* (Crown, 1951).

W. Van T. Clark, *The Ox-Bow Incident* (Random House, 1940).

W. Van T. Clark, *The Track of the Cat* (Random House, 1949).

R. G. Cleland, *This Reckless Breed of Men* (Knopf, 1950).

H. L. Davis, *Honey in the Horn* (Harper, 1935).

H. L. Davis, *Winds of Morning* (Morrow, 1951).

F. Eaton, *Pistol Pete* (Little, Brown, 1952).

E. Fergusson, *New Mexico* (Knopf, 1951).

E. Fergusson, *Our Southwest* (Knopf, 1940).

H. McCracken, *Portrait of the Old West* (McGraw-Hill, 1952).

F. Waters, *The Colorado* (Rinehart, 1946).

F. Waters, *Masked Gods* (University of New Mexico, 1950).

Oxford and Its Press

ALL great cities, and all great universities, are like people: they are individuals, and can never be fully understood without personal knowledge. Have you ever read a description of Paris or New York which came anywhere near the truth? Elliot Paul, and Delius, and Jules Romains have done much to draw Paris; but whenever I am there I see much which they have omitted. E. B. White and Scott Fitzgerald and many others have tried to state the essence of New York. They have not failed; but they have not fully succeeded. Well, Oxford—both city and university—is like that. It can scarcely be described; it must be known. But also, it cannot be understood at all without some description given by someone who knows it. Therefore, although by definition my attempt is bound to fail, I should like to attempt to tell you something about Oxford—one of the three cities I love most in the whole world. (The other two I have already named.)

I shall begin with the worst. Oxford used to be a small handsome university town. It is now a large ugly industrial city, with a small and still beautiful university quarter tucked inside it. This has happened within our own lifetime, and it has been an unparalleled disaster. When I went up to Oxford in 1929 it was still beautiful, although the encroachments of factories and cheap houses had begun. When I left, in 1937, it was already suffering gravely; and now the process has gone much farther. The authorities of the main colleges have almost given up the struggle to keep out the roar of traffic, the dirt and smells which accompany buses and trucks everywhere: they are concentrating now on keeping their buildings from being shaken to pieces. The beauties of Oxford, like St. John's Garden and Tom Quad in Christ Church, used to be single notes in a rich symphony of beauty; now they are tiny oases in a spreading desert of noise and ugliness. Some of our own universities here have already gone part of the same way, and I devoutly pray that it will not happen to others. Princeton, for instance, is still absolutely delightful; but the last time I was there I heard the ominous word DEVELOPMENT and I saw the hateful monster TRAFFIC, snorting and hooting and hurrying and trumpeting, polluting the calm air, the quiet and lovely buildings.

That is the worst about Oxford, and it is very sad. Like so many damaging processes, it is apparently irreversible. I have no objection to change when it means improvement, or the substitution of one good for another; but change which is deterioration fills me with a sense of irreparable loss. Something has been killed. We have lost, forever lost, that being whom Matthew Arnold called 'adorable dreamer,' the gracious thoughtful presence with her crown of towers.

In spite of its physical deterioration, Oxford remains a

mighty spiritual force. The University is more active than ever before. All kinds of creative work are being carried on, with greater intensity than any living man remembers. And this is not merely a short-lived and febrile intensity. Long-term projects of great importance have been carried out, and others are coming to fruition. Many of these have been fostered by the Oxford University Press. At this moment, for instance, it is producing a Latin dictionary. Now, there is no good Latin dictionary in existence in any language. The one we use in America was produced about seventy years ago by two Columbia men, on the basis of an earlier work by the German scholar Freund. It is not bad, but it is partly wrong and partly obsolete. In Munich the German universities, now much assisted by money from America and, I think, UNESCO, have for over half a century been slowly printing a tremendous work which is meant to contain analyses of every meaning of every word in Latin, with millions of examples; but it is not yet half finished. So, a good number of years ago, the Oxford Press determined to make a really complete and valid Latin dictionary. They had already published the only good Greek lexicon in any language, the magnificent Liddell & Scott, revised by Sir Henry Stuart Jones and Roderick McKenzie. A thing like that needs enormous investment in time, in money, in ungrudging unpaid research, in hope and tenacity of purpose. The Press made these investments. They found a devoted group of scholars to assemble the material, and to edit it; they found others to do sectional research and to contribute the results; they sent out, to scholars all over the world, a prospectus and a specimen page, asking for criticisms and improvements. The work is well in hand now, and it will be completed within the foreseeable future. It will certainly be a success, in the long-term sense; but it will take many years to return the investment which the Press has sunk in it.

And that is only one of many large co-operative enterprises

sponsored by the Press: *The Oxford History of England, The Oxford Companion to Music, The Oxford Companion to the Theatre, The Oxford Classical Dictionary* (which took fifteen years), *The Oxford English Dictionary* itself. All these things are expensive to build; they need long planning and elaborately supervised execution; but they are meant to last, and they do last.

In a certain sense, the Press is not merely a branch of the University of Oxford, but one of its most important activities. The University, as such, hardly exists. It has hardly any buildings, and scarcely any permanent officials. It is a sort of emanation of the separate colleges—there are about thirty in all, which have existed for varying lengths of time, between seven years and seven centuries. It holds examinations and gives degrees; but it scarcely teaches. The teaching, and nine-tenths of the work of the university of Oxford, is done by and in the colleges.

You will ask what is the purpose of these separate colleges? Exeter and Lincoln, Balliol and Trinity, Christ Church and New College and Merton and St. John's, what function do they really perform? They all provide house room for the students (called undergraduates), of course, and cook meals for them: that was their original purpose. But what higher function have they?

They have several. At one time they were designed to give hospitality to men from different parts of Britain, like the Nations who made up the University of Paris. Jesus College is still a favorite of Welshmen; Balliol was founded by a Scottish prince and has bred many Scotsmen (among others, Adam Smith the economist), although brilliant Englishmen have always been allowed inside, too; Exeter welcomes people from the southwest of England. Then the colleges also have connections with the big English schools; sometimes a school and a college were founded by the same man, as New College and Winchester were founded by William of Wykeham: sometimes there are special scholarships from one school to one special college.

Then another function of the separate colleges is to give individual tuition to the undergraduates. A small society—if it is properly endowed—can have a tutor for each of the principal subjects, chemistry, history, law, and so forth; and can arrange to give the young men individual tuition for many hours each week, with individual supervision and advice throughout their college career. A big institution like a University cannot do this, without creating rather bogus and impersonal organizations to do it.

The separate colleges also have their own libraries. No doubt it would be possible for a central university library to provide enough reference books for all the undergraduates studying every subject; but it would be clumsy and uneconomic. In a small college library one can easily allow the necessary books to circulate year after year, or at worst to be reserved on a table, where the readers will all know one another.

The existence of separate colleges also makes it possible for far more of the young men to engage in sports. Only twenty or twenty-five people can reach the University's first team; but when there are thirty colleges, each with one or more teams, practically everyone can play. The hottest competition is in football and rowing, which occupy the two terms of that interminably dreary British winter. In the summer comes cricket, which is like baseball played by men who are either very polite or very ill, and sometimes both; but at its best it is supremely decorative, one of the prettiest of games, combining the charm of a ballet with that of a Wedgwood vase.

But the chief function of the separate colleges in Oxford is to provide different focuses of thought. The mind of humanity is very various, full of strange outcrops and unexpected elaborations and differences of emphasis and conflicts which sometimes become harmonies and sometimes remain forever as polar tests of strength. Therefore it needs variety in which to express itself. One single organization, with one single unified structure, is probably a good thing for making money; but not for thinking thoughts or making works of art. No man is as great as the Logos, the voice of reason. No single thought-out organization is as rich as the work of reason, and can give shelter to the many different shapes which reason may take. The purpose of a university is not to arrange and control thought, but to fertilize and stimulate and encourage thought. This can hardly be done by a monolithic organization; but it can be done by a vague and anomalously organized and madly diverse collection of colleges—the more different the better.

(The undergraduates of Harvard have recently been organized in a similar way—into a set of Houses, each of which has a Master and a library of its own, and all of which differ in their characters, their ambitions, and their purposes; so also in Yale; and perhaps in other universities too. I might say that when I had the pleasure of visiting the library of one House at Harvard, I really thought I was back in Oxford. It was 6:30 in the evening, and the room was quite empty.)

The differences between the colleges of Oxford are not artificial. They are like the differences between people—the result of the accidents of birth and the policies of nurture. They are displayed in the differences between the college buildings. At one extreme there is tiny little Corpus Christi—the front quadrangle would just make a good-sized garden for a house in the country. At the other, there is Christ Church, whose front quadrangle is nearly 100 yards square, and has a cathedral church tucked away in one corner. Among the college buildings there are some hideous atrocities, which I dare not even name in case I should call them up to memory; some mediocrities; some eccentricities; some failures; and some startling successes in every vein from thirteenth century Gothic through fine seventeenth-century baroque to twentieth-century electic. St. John's has one quadrangle built by Archbishop Laud, which combines the battlements of Gothic with the curved arches and statuesque decorations of the Renaissance, and so, like Oxford itself, looks forward and back at once.

The history of all these beautiful things has been well described, with attractive pictures from all periods, by Christopher Hobhouse, in a book called *Oxford as It Was and as It Is Today,* published by the Press and by Batsford in 1939 or so. It has been supplemented by Arthur Woolley's book *Oxford, University & City,* which contains less text and more beautiful pictures. Such books remind us that architecture is the neglected sister among the Muses. If I had ever built a fine church, or a college, or even a quadrangle, I should want to have my name on it. But who knows the names of the architects of many of the finest buildings in the world? Some of them were only workmen. For instance, the exquisite fanvaulting of Christ Church Hall was created by a stonemason, long after fan-vaulting (which is a Gothic idea) was officially obsolete. We know practically nothing about him, except that he was a genius. He came from London, and his name was Smith.

What about the education given by these colleges and supervised, in a rather absent-minded, elderly-uncle sort of way, by the University? It can be outlined, it can be sketched, in the words *incompleteness, inquiry,* and *individualism.* This means that when a young man goes to Oxford he is taught that he is an important individual, with his own abilities and his own defects, which have to be brought out or amended; he is told that neither he nor his teachers nor the so-called experts elsewhere know everything, that they do not know things definitely, and that they do not even know things immutably, from one decade to the next; and he is assured that every single thing which is said to him or by him may be a lie, or a mistake, or an overstatement, or a misuse of words. This sounds discouraging, but it is not. It helps the young, it saves them from the feeling of being pressed down under an enormous stone, the weight of centuries of authority and truth, the feeling that everything has been discovered long ago. There is no authority. Believe no one. Your tutor tells you about Plato. Begin by disbelieving the tutor. Go on to question Plato. Say to yourself, 'What did Plato *mean* when he said that knowledge of absolutes was recollection?' and then ask, 'Was he right in saying so?' Think. Think for yourself. Remember the tradition of the centuries of scholars who have made your own thought possible; but remember that they were your equals, and think as their friend, as their rival.

It is a splendid education, one of the finest educational systems which has ever been worked out, in the long and usually disastrously boring history of education throughout the world.

The Oxford University Press is part of that system. And it is something else, much else, besides. I once asked the Secretary of the Press why it was such a fine institution. (It sounds a naïve question, but I had just been looking through its standing catalogue and I had seen about 300 books which

I wanted badly to buy: it was hard to think of them all coming out of one firm, however far-sighted.) He thought for a while, and then he answered, 'I think it's because we do so many things which people feel we ought—as a University Press—not to do!' And as one looks over the catalogue, one sees that is true. Many of the books it publishes have nothing closely to do with the University of Oxford at all. Many of them will sell comparatively few copies in Oxford and many thousands in London and New York and Toronto and Delhi and Sydney. Many of them are rather frivolous, and some are so extremely highly specialized that they would normally be put out by a learned society, the Association of Entomologists in its Annual, rather than a firm. But, unlike most other university presses, the Oxford Press believes that its duty is both to serve as the printer and publisher of the University for its own purposes, and to bring out and encourage books which will communicate to a much wider, to a world-wide public, the kind of information and inspiration which springs most strongly from a university. This does not mean only Great Books—although it does mean Great Books, too. It means small, friendly manuals of information for intelligent people who cannot go to the University but who want the same kind of reliability and responsibility as one expects from a university teacher.

The Press began nearly 500 years ago simply as the printing shop for Oxford University. In 1632 it branched out. It acquired the hope and prayer of every publishing house, a permanent best seller: this was the Holy Bible. In order to print and to distribute the Bible, the Press acquired a warehouse in London. In course of time this grew into a separate department, publishing books which would not interest Oxford alone, or which would not interest Oxford primarily: so that now there are two Oxford Presses, one in Oxford, called the Clarendon Press after the Clarendon Buildings where its printing shop used to be, and the other in London, publishing a broader range of books. The American branch makes a third, which grew up in the same way. In 1896 a branch was opened in New York to organize the distribution of the Oxford Bibles, and of any other Oxford Press books which would be likely to sell. Gradually it acquired powers and interests of its own, and now it has its own policies and its own staff. More than half the books which it produces are selected and printed and published in the United States. It is rather tricky to follow all this, but you will have noticed that it falls into the same pattern as the divergence of the colleges in Oxford: the human mind is various, tastes differ, appetites and needs vary from place to place, so let us give them all room to move.

The finances of the Press are a secret, known only to the Secretary and the Delegates. The Delegates are the real governing body of the whole world-wide organization. They are simply Oxford dons, chosen for their taste and judgment. The Delegates represent the University of Oxford, which is the owner and sole shareholder of the entire business. They get no pay whatever, and they have to do a good deal of difficult and expert work; their only reward—their only material reward—is that they get a copy of every book published by the Press during their term of office. It may sound sentimental, but it is true, to say that much of the work done for the Press is done for love: simply for the love of learning and of good books.

The Press pays its authors well: not too well, but well enough, and fairly enough. And I am credibly informed that it never asks an author for a subsidy. As you know, that is one of the tortures of being a scholar in an unfrequented field. You spend ten years writing a manual of malacology, with illustrations, and then you send it to a publisher, who replies that it will have a very small sale and that he will need an advance of $10,000 before he can think of producing it. You can apply to the American Council of Learned Societies, I suppose; or mortgage your mother; but it is discouraging. Well now, I understand that the Press either refuses a book, or else undertakes to publish it; and offers you the due share in the profits if it should sell. Lots of them cannot sell many copies. The catalogue contains some items of which I cannot even understand the titles: for instance, two simple little jobs called, respectively, *Geodesy* and *Hyperconjugation*; and there are others, such as a *Catalogue of Ethiopian Manuscripts in the Bodleian* and a list of *Breeding Birds of Kashmir,* whose appeal must be rather limited. But the Press invests the vast labor and material required for these books just because it thinks they ought to be published, and it makes up the loss on such books by the very popular *Companions* and *Dictionaries* and by the many much broader works which take its name all over the world. Last year, the Secretary tells me, it sent out *nine million books.*

As well as the various English Dictionaries and Fowler's *Modern English Usage,* the Press puts out several books which are meant to help beginning authors. If you have ever even edited a college magazine, you will know how vague people are about spelling unusual words, about punctuation, about foreign phrases and accents, and how hard they find it to correct proofs. The Press has experienced this for centuries, and so it has produced an *Authors' and Printers' Dictionary,* by F. H. Collins, which is now in its eighth edition, and ought to be on every professional writer's table. In 1893 it produced a modest little set of *Rules for Compositors and Readers at the University Press,* which is now in about its fortieth edition, and is also invaluable. (Stationary? Stationery? What is the plural of grotto?) There is a longer work on the whole process of getting a book printed, called *Manuscript & Proof,* by Benbow, which I have not seen. And Miss Margaret Nicholson, of the New York branch, has prepared a charming little booklet simply called *An Author's Style Book,* which begins with the words, sad, but true, and little understood:

> Poor copy is expensive to set, causes waste in production time, and is a source of author's alteration costs.

Well: we have come a long way: from the great University and its colleges to the care of commas and the cost of proof corrections. But they are interconnected. I remember once I traveled to the south of France to look at a manuscript. It had been written in the ninth century, by a good honest scribe who did not scrimp his ink or hurry his pen. But there was one passage in which I had long been aware of a difficulty. I turned eagerly to that. Surely this manuscript would tell me the plain, clear truth? or else an honest mistake? No. Just at that place, some time back in the year 850 or so, my scribe had been tired, or he had not taken enough ink into his writing room, or he had been interrupted, or one of the many temptations of the flesh had assailed him, or perhaps he had heard outside, as many of the writers of our best manuscripts could hear, the yells and screams and explosions and conflagrations which meant that another bloody war had approached his study; but anyhow he had written the line badly, and weakly, and it could not be clearly read. I did not blame him, for he was a good scribe; but I was sorry for the loss. Now, that is why good printers work hard at making their books, and that is why responsible publishers think carefully about choosing and producing their books. They know —some consciously, many instinctively—that if you do a good job it will last, and that if it lasts it will be a part of civilization, which is man's effort to outlive his own life and to assert something which can be called a permanent set of values. And they know the odd fact that a poem lasts longer than a city, that a thought will outlive an empire:

> Not marble, nor the gilded monuments
> Of princes, shall outlive this powerful rime . . .

So said Shakespeare, and it is true; but it is true only because great poems are printed again and again from age to age, and are taught by faithful teachers who understand that most of the present comes from the past.

From World to World

———————————

MOST of us rather despise scientific fiction. In fact, most of it is despicable. Sometimes it is also frightening. The worst thing about it is that whenever it looks into the future it shows us something like the present, only worse. Sometimes, as you read 'scientifiction' stories or look at the miscalled 'comics' which deal with the scientifuture (or *are* they miscalled, after all?), you feel that the future will be even more repulsive than the present—because it will be inhabited entirely by mad scientists like Dr. Klaus Fuchs, noble but impotent father-symbols, and hot-rod jet pilots aged eighteen, sometimes assisted by boy mechanics aged twelve, and plump young pilotesses who look like a cross between roller-skating champions and drum-majorettes.

But that is because these books are not about science, and

not really about the future. The science in them is negligible. It has no factories behind it, no research, no deep philosophical understanding, no basis in universities and research laboratories, and no real roots in society—whereas genuine science is the work of a community backing up a series of great thinkers and translating their thought into act. Most of the scientifiction books I have seen remind me of my first thriller, which I got when I was five years old. Instead of Rocket Roger and Colonel Universe, its hero was a little chap called King Pippin. He had a magic pair of wings (now they would be a 'space suit'), I think he had a cap of invisibility (now it would be an 'atomic dissolver'), and I know he had a magic sword (now it would be a 'neutron spray'); and he fought a series of dreadful giants and supramundane monarchs, ending with The Mighty King of Kings (not God, but 'Mr. Solar System'). His difficulties were tremendous; but he always won. It was only a few years ago that I found out who he was. He was a real prince. He was a man who had been transformed into an invincible myth. He was Pepin le Bref, father of Charlemagne—who died in A.D. 768, over a thousand years before I read about him. All that time, he had passed down through fairy stories, the dreams of children, and the retentive imaginations of tale-tellers. That is the world to which most scientifiction books belong: the world of medieval fable, full of robber barons, gallant knights, fiendish sorcerers, giants and dwarfs, dragons and Valkyries.

Of course there are many good serious non-fiction books about the exploration of space. Several brilliant ones have been produced in the last two or three years. But that is not everything, for, as you will agree, we do not fully understand any region of experience until we can translate it into art or music, poetry or fiction. What is lacking? Why are nearly all scientifiction books so childish?

Surely it is because they lack moral and intellectual content. The real point of astronomy, and of the contemplation and exploration of other worlds, is that it raises human beings high above their ordinary levels of thought as well as action. Therefore, in a story about people involved in such adventures we must somehow show them confronted with new moral and intellectual problems, and growing mentally and morally in order to solve them. If there are intelligent beings in other worlds, then they will be like us in some things and radically different from us in others; and will they inhabit the same *moral* universe, with similar conceptions of duty, honor, and kindness, or will their moral code be quite different, differing as widely from ours as that of the headhunting Melanesians?

And surely it is impossible to think hard about exploring space without seeing that it is in essence a religious problem. For it is a problem of ultimate significance. Is there a Creator of the Universe? If so, what was his purpose in creating it? In particular, what is his relation to us? Are we its only inhabitants, the only beings in thousands of millions of stars and planets who know him and worship him? Is all the rest merely what the Persian astronomer Omar Khayyam called it, a 'magic shadow-show'? merely a collection of physical equations made visible? If so, then surely the Creator who gave us reason intends us to go out from this little planet and not only explore but occupy more of the cosmos. But if not, if there are other intelligent beings on other planets, many races of them, then what is their knowledge of God? what is their religion? and how is it related to our own religion or religions, which all seem to be so earthbound, so concentrated on the events of one small planet revolving round a secondary star?

Hard problems, these. We feel them hard even as we talk about them. How much harder must it be to put them into a work of the imagination! Whoever does so must somehow have solved them in his own mind first; and few of us are capable of doing that.

There is one writer who has. He has written a number of good books, several of them quite famous. But his three scientification romances are those which interest me particularly. If you don't know them I should like to introduce you to them. If you do I should like to share your appreciation of them.

He is C. S. Lewis, Clive Staples Lewis, and the books are all published by Macmillan. Their names are odd, perhaps too odd to be successful; but they are poetic. The first is, *Out of the Silent Planet.* The second is *Perelandra.* The third is *That Hideous Strength.* They came out during and just after the war, at intervals during the 'forties. I have read them all half a dozen times or more: they haunt me.

Lewis himself is an Oxford don, about fifty years old, of Anglo-Irish stock. He was apparently a hedonist and an atheist of the variety which was so common in the 1920's: you know, LIFE HAS NO MEANING WHAT DOES IT ALL MATTER? LET'S HAVE A GOOD TIME WHILE WE LAST. But he has too much brain and too good a heart for that. He underwent a religious conversion and is now a fervent Christian. In addition, he became a friend of a remarkable poet and mystic called Charles Williams, himself the author of seven or eight romantic novels about the problem of good and evil. Lewis was known as a scholar for his work on medieval poetry, but he first entered public view during the worst of the war with a splendid fantasy called *The Screwtape Letters.* His novels appeared after that, and have many hearty admirers.

They are all based on a picture of the universe which is new to me, but which I suppose must be orthodox Christian mystical doctrine. I find it both terrifying and beautiful.

Consider one of the great questions about the universe and its creator—whether we are its only inhabitants, or there are others too, who know and worship God? The answer to that question, for Lewis, involves answers to other painfully hard questions: why are men wicked? why did the first man, in Paradise, fall into sin? why did Jesus come to save us? is there a Devil, and what is his power over us? Here is his answer.

The universe is all good, all happy, and all populated by spirits who know and serve God. It is not empty space, traversed by wandering comets and punctuated by foolish explosions. It is richly inhabited by intelligent and sentient beings and pervaded throughout by the presence of God. Properly seen, or rather mystically experienced, the entire cosmos is a magnificent dance of energy in which God is adored by all his creatures.

There is one exception. That is this world and its satellite, the moon. Many ages ago, long before the creation of mankind, one of the mightiest of angels revolted against God. He was cast out of the great fellowship of spirits. He became Satan, the Tempter, the Devil. He still exists and works. His greatest triumph after the original revolt was his invasion of this world. It was he who tempted and perverted the newly created human beings, Adam and Eve. In a sense, he really rules this planet, and that is why the Son of God had to come into human life and be crucified, in order to re-establish God's power here. Now the world is, as it were, a battle zone. This is the front line of the struggle between good and evil, between the Devil and God. When the struggle approaches its final decision, human beings will be of small account—they will be like ants on a battlefield. But until then, every time we do a cruel action or entertain an evil thought, we are taking part in that battle: and on the wrong side.

This makes remarkably good sense, doesn't it? Much mysticism does not, but this does. Most of us have felt that the history of humanity shows so many awful violences and perversions, war, slavery, torture, and lust, that the world could not be governed directly by God. Most of us have felt that God's power is here, but that it is constantly offset by some other power, and that we can trace the struggle of superhuman forces, evil and good, not only in the history of our race, but even within our own soul.

And some of us have felt that it would be not only useless but even wicked for us to explore space and to invade other planets if we were to do no more than to transplant to them the dreary lusts and hatreds of our own. It is bad enough to occupy the plains of Africa and convert them into a battleground for black men, brown men, and white men; but it would surely be a sin to invade another world in order to exterminate its inhabitants and then start fighting for its possessions and exploitation as we have done elsewhere. If we did, says C. S. Lewis, we should in fact be carrying out the Devil's strategy. This is his base of operations, this world, right here. Other planets are occupied by happy unsuspecting creatures and defended by their guardians, the angels whom men have known as Michael or as Mars or as Mercury and Jupiter. Yet if men can gain a footing on them, particularly men who are clever, treacherous, remorseless, and greedy, their happiness will be destroyed, and they will either fall into the power of the Devil or at least become battlegrounds as this world is.

That is the basis of Lewis's first story. *Out of the Silent Planet* tells how two brilliant and covetous scientists invaded Mars, taking with them a comparative stranger as a potential sacrifice; how they found three quite different species of inhabitants, all unlike mankind in appearance but all happy, peaceful, and intelligent; how they attempted to kill some and dominate them, but were—largely by the help of the stranger—defeated and driven away.

The second story, *Perelandra,* is even stranger. The Devil shows his strategy more clearly: indeed it is implied that he has actually mastered and possessed one of the scientists. For the story is a re-enactment of the temptation of Eve in the garden. On the planet Venus, which is younger than we are, a man and a woman have been created. They are the first; they are its Adam and its Eve; although they have not come together yet. Speaking through Weston the scientist, Satan tempts this beautiful creature—not to eat an apple but to 'know good and evil,' instead of good alone. He tells her story after story of passionate lovers and noble but misunderstood women in this world; he shows her how to make pretty, useless clothes and admire herself—all in order to plunge her into the state of perpetual doubt and revolt which will ruin her marriage and begin to wreck her soul.

And he is beginning to succeed: but Ransom, the stranger of the other book, has been brought in by angelic power to counteract him. First, by talk, he strengthens the woman's resolution; and finally he attacks and overpowers the tempter. All this takes place in a beautifully described setting of young, fresh charm: floating islands, exquisite birds and fruit, perfect harmony between animals and human beings, something like Eden itself.

The third story, *That Hideous Strength,* changes the scene of the struggle to this world; and although it is brilliant, too, it often passes the point where mysticism changes into sheer nonsense. I cannot recommend it so highly; but if you read the first two you will want to read it also, and if you do you will long remember the blood-sacrifice to the severed head which can still speak and suffer.

Well, this is strange stuff, isn't it? But moving: poetic and religious at once. Nor can we dismiss it as nonsense. Which would you rather inhabit—a universe full of conscious beings joined in harmonious service to their Creator, or a universe empty of everything except ourselves and a few chemical or physical reactions? To live in the second would really be nonsense, for it would be meaningless. Man's life has significance only if it is part of a larger and a nobler order of things; and science even at its most brilliant is only a door through which we pass to reach that order.

————

C. S. Lewis, *Mere Christianity* (Macmillan, 1952).
　　　　Out of the Silent Planet (Macmillan, 1943).
　　　　Perelandra (Macmillan, 1944).
　　　　The Screwtape Letters (Macmillan, 1943).
　　　　That Hideous Strength (Macmillan, 1946).

A Guide to Oxford

THERE are many cities in the world, but only a few of them are magical. Only a few of them have changed from a crowd of buildings into a Person, a Spirit, a Presence which is unique. At least three cities in this country have done so: New York, San Francisco, and New Orleans . . . perhaps more. In Asia, too, there are such cities—Peiping with the palace at its center, and Damascus. And there are many in Europe: Paris, Florence, Seville, many more, all different, all beautiful, all lovable, all beloved.

Among them, the European city I know best is Oxford. It was once very beautiful: and at its center the buildings are still exquisite; but in our lifetime it has been all but wrecked by overcrowding, industrialization, the addition of huge factories and cheap houses, materialism, and irrelevant through traffic, so that now it is worse than Cambridge, Massachusetts, and infinitely worse than its quieter sister, the English Cambridge.

However, its spirit has not changed: that is, the spirit of its University has not changed. I suppose there are many thousands of people who live and work in Oxford just as though it were an ordinary mill town, and think of the University, if at all, as a sort of eccentric Latin Quarter. But within the walls of the colleges, and on the river, and in the great Bodleian Library, and at University functions, the personality of Oxford maintains itself, with all its dignity, grace, eccentricity, and charm.

I have just been reading a delightful book which both tries to define and describe that charm and, in doing so, expresses and embodies it. This is called *To Teach the Senators Wisdom, or An Oxford Guide-Book*. Its author is J. C. Masterman, the Provost of Worcester College. In 1933 he wrote a story of murder and detection in Oxford, called *An Oxford Tragedy*: full of sharp character-drawing and ingenuity, if not of the tragic sense. And now he has done something more difficult, something which only O. Henry and E. B. White have been able to do for New York: he has described the place in such a way that you understand it, and want to learn more of it, and see by his very manner what sort of spirit informs it.

It is not an ordinary guide-book: naturally; an ordinary guide-book would be quite wrong. It has a story, with a surprise ending; and it is told largely in conversations which are both learned and witty, because Oxford is carried on largely by learned and witty conversations. It opens in the Senior Common Room—that is, the dining room reserved for the Fellows, corresponding to the Faculty Club—of a fictitious but typical Oxford college, during the summer vacation. Eight of the Fellows are still in residence: a retired historian, very old, nearly eighty, whose memory for the origin and meaning of traditions is far-reaching; the chaplain; the tutor in Law, rather hard and bitter and edgy; the Dean, friendly and loquacious; the Bursar (he looks after the finances of the college and supervises its estates and investments, for remember that the Oxford colleges were not founded and endowed primarily to teach the young—they were founded for the pursuit of learning and most of them still pursue it); then there is the tutor in Classics, who has already been a professor at a Scottish university but has returned to Oxford; the tutor in Modern Languages, who has been a diplomat and then, during the war, a brilliant soldier; finally, a pensive scientist, who hates conversation.

As the book opens, the Dean is discussing his plan to write a guide-book to Oxford. He consults the others, asking them what must be in it and what can be left out. But before the plan can go farther, an external force intervenes, and takes it out of the realm of discussion. One of the great benefactors of the college, a rich but rather irksome extrovert, writes to say that three American friends of his, who showed him great hospitality when he was in Washington, are coming to visit Oxford, and that he relies on the Fellows to show them all that is most interesting and most valuable, in short, to tell them what Oxford is. There is not much time to prepare, only a few days. Then the Senators—for naturally Sir John would have met only the most important men in Washington—will arrive. The guide-book must be prepared at once, in the form of notes. At once, the Fellows must decide what their guests are to be shown and told.

And so, in several evenings of discussion, sometimes laced by charming stories, and sometimes sharpened by brisk arguments, the eight men work out what they think are the essentials of Oxford, to be shown to intelligent strangers who visit the University with an open mind. It is impossible to read these chapters without learning a great deal about Oxford, whoever you are, however well you may know it or however vague you may be about it.

The Fellows begin logically by arguing with each other about the purpose and the organization of the University and its relation to the separate colleges which make it up; how it is governed, in fact, what it is for. (One of the things I like about the book is that it does not idealize the Fellows as individuals, and does not forget the sharply critical attitude which, as intellectuals thrown much together in an atmosphere of keen discussion, they are apt to generate toward one another. For instance, just at this point the Dean suggests that the Law Tutor should tell the Senators the facts about the purpose of the University, since 'his legal training will enable him to define precisely, and his great knowledge of the subject will enable him to be short.' To which one of the other Fellows replies, 'I should have thought that that would have made him deucedly long,' and the author comments, 'Trower seldom missed an opportunity of stating the obvious.' Delightful, isn't it? I can hear the very tone of voice in which these remarks were made.) This particular chapter contains a revealing story about Roosevelt—Teddy Roosevelt, not his young cousin. He was being shown round Christ Church, the largest and noblest of the colleges; and both he and his guide were profoundly bored. 'This,' the guide would say, pointing to a picture, 'is by Reynolds and a very fine example of his work, and this by Romney and much admired.' And the President was saying 'Oh' at intervals, without much conviction. In time the guide came to a double row of pictures in the Senior Common Room. 'There,' he said, 'are portraits of members of the House who became Governors-General or Viceroys of India—Wellesley, and Dalhousie, and Aberdeen, and all the rest of them.' 'What!' said Roosevelt, 'what! Do you tell me that all those great governors came from this one college?' 'Indeed I do,' said the Fellow who was guiding him. And then the whole scene changed, and he could hardly keep pace with all the President's questions and enquiries. In fact, Roosevelt saw in a flash that Oxford was not just the museum of antiquities which he had supposed it to be, but a nursery of great men.

After discussing how they shall tell the Senators what the University is, and what it is for, the Fellows go on to decide what they shall be shown: what are the sights. They agree that the Senators must be taken into the most graceful quadrangle in Oxford: the Canterbury Quadrangle in St. John's College. It is an exquisite piece of building, which has been exquisite for nearly 400 years: it has crenelations which are Gothic and slender arches which are the best Renaissance style. Archbishop Laud, who had been President of the College, paid for the entire cost of the building himself, and, as the Fellows said, 'Its very stones gave forth'—and they still give forth—'music to his glory.' But apart from beauties, there are things of interest to show: historically memorable, or simply odd. The scientist thinks two windows in the School of Pathology may be the most beautiful view in the world: for behind those two windows Florey and his team worked on the discovery of penicillin. And the classicist remembers a place which will take you into Lewis Carroll's Oxford. It is possible to travel below the entire central city of Oxford, in a canoe, along an underground stream. You go in beside the Castle, and voyage in more or less darkness for twenty minutes, and then emerge away down by Christ Church. Perhaps that was the stream along which Alice rowed with the sheep. Anyhow, the classicist says that he once made the journey along with three other men; he says how odd it was to hear the traffic rumbling and booming above his head at the central crossroads while he drifted beneath; and he remembers that he and his friends must have looked extremely eccentric when they emerged—two of them in morning coats and top hats, because it was on the day of Encaenia, corresponding to Commencement—slowly and with immense dignity, in a canoe, from an underground stream closely resembling, if not identical with, a sewer, into the calm and formal atmosphere of Christ Church Meadows. They were as unexpected, and as traditional, as a unicorn.

After this, the Fellows go on to discuss learning and teaching. This part is full of good stories—especially when they talk about academic discipline and examinations. I remember one myself about the formerly universal preliminary examination in Holy Scripture. A large, beefy athlete, who had read neither the Bible nor any other complicated book, was to be examined on his knowledge of the Scriptures. He had learned a number of essential facts. When the time came, he found that his paper contained one crucial question: *Name and Describe the Major and the Minor Hebrew Prophets.* He thought for a while: that was one list he had not learned. So he wrote, 'Far be it from me to make such invidious distinctions. It would be more fitting in this place to give a list of the kings of Israel and the kings of Judah'—which he then proceeded to do.

There is a much better story than that in the book: an agonizing story, for anyone who has ever been through an examination: about St. Paul and the city of Ephesus . . . There is also a yarn about an undergraduate who was stopped on his way to a vaudeville theater by the proctor. (The proctor is one of the dons, an instructor or what not, who is serving for a year as the head of the University police.) The proctor suspected this youth because he had a large parcel concealed under his coat. The young man produced it. It was an enormous fish: uncooked. The proctor felt sure that the fish would shortly be thrown onto the stage, in front of some particularly repulsive comedian at the East Oxford Theatre; but he could not assume that. So he said, with calm civility, 'May I ask why you are carrying this turbot?' 'Sir,' said the undergraduate, 'I thought it was a sound thing to have about me.' Now, to a policeman who was also a philosopher, what answer could be better?

And so the Fellows continue to discuss the University which they know and love. At the end of their discussions, the visitors from Washington are announced. They turn out not to be Senators at all. They turn out to be—no, I must not spoil the denouement for you: it should be read. But at the end, as we look back over the book, we find that the conversations have not only helped to clarify the essentials about Oxford, but themselves represented most of those essentials.

For instance, one of the main principles of Oxford is this: *Do not change the beautiful.* So, right at the beginning, the scientist points out that the Senior Common Room ought to have fluorescent lighting, instead of candles in silver candlesticks on the walnut table. And the oldest of the Fellows, old Winn, cries, 'What utter folly: you cannot be serious. Fluorescent lighting. I don't know what fluorescent lighting is, but I dislike it—I dislike it very much indeed. I abominate it.' And, for a seventeenth-century room and in a seventeenth-century room, he is right. I wish we had such beautiful rooms nowadays.

Of course there is a great deal of wit and humor, for, after all, they are the natural by-product of intellectual activity, in association with youth. The finest example in recent years is recorded here. One of the undergraduates hired the Town Hall, announced that Dr. Emil Busch, the eminent specialist in psychology, would lecture on the latest developments in that science, and sent out tickets all over Oxford. A large audience turned out, including many distinguished dons. The undergraduate, aged twenty, came on suitably disguised; he lectured for an hour in a mixture of double talk and a fruity Viennese accent *mit Schlagobers*; the audience listened with attention; and he sent them away, puzzled but interested. An hour later, he released the full story to the papers. A magnificent hoax, magnificent.

The book also contains just a trace of—I shall not say snobbishness, for that is a universal vice; but the specially Oxford assumption of 'effortless superiority.' (I used to think this was entirely reserved to Oxford, until I met some Yale men.) The best guide to acquiring this attitude at home, without the expense and trouble of going to college, can be found in the works of Stephen Potter: see his new manual, *One-Upmanship,* published by Holt. And the consolation of university teachers is that those who do not profit intellectually from four years at college at least emerge with the consciousness of being permanently, in *one* aspect of life, *One Up*.

But most of all the book emphasizes the best kind of education: *the development of each person's individuality to its full power,* through hard, but not mechanical, learning; through respect for his own special powers and interests; through the play of emotion as well as intellect; through training in social and political life as well as the life of the mind, and through competition and collaboration with people from many lands and many groups.

To Teach the Senators Wisdom is, itself, a good example

of the half-serious, half-humorous eccentricity, the half-rebellious, half-poetic independence, which have marked Oxford and some of her best products. As Hemingway once wrote, there is a lot of difference between a serious book and a solemn book. This is serious; but it is witty, and indirect, and ironic; and, without being solemn, very wise.

J. C. Masterman, *To Teach the Senators Wisdom; or An Oxford Guide Book* (Oxford, 1952).

A new book, full of humor, charm, and intimate knowledge of Oxford, produced by two people who have loved the University for a long lifetime, is *Came to Oxford* (Oxford, 1953), with text by Gertrude Bone and illustrations by Muirhead Bone.

Sailing to Byzantium

Histroy is a strange experience. The world is quite small now; but history is large and deep. Sometimes you can go much farther by sitting in your own home and reading a book of history, than by getting onto a ship or an airplane and traveling a thousand miles. When you go to Mexico City through space, you find it a sort of cross between modern Madrid and modern Chicago, with additions of its own; but if you go to Mexico City through history, back only 500 years, you will find it as distant as though it were on another planet: inhabited by cultivated barbarians, sensitive and cruel, highly organized and still in the Copper Age, a collection of startling, of unbelievable contrasts.

There is one such world, one historically distant planet, which very few of us have ever visited. This is Byzantium.

The city which was called Byzantium is now called Constantinople, or rather Istanbul, in modern Turkey. But the civilization called Byzantine was the Roman empire: it was the eastern section of the Roman empire, its oldest and its most culturally fertile area, the Greek part of the Greco-Roman world. From another point of view, equally important, Byzantium was the Roman empire refounded as a Christian empire. And do you know that it survived until just 500 years ago, until 1453—nearly 1000 years after the western Roman empire had crumbled into fragments? It still existed, and it still called itself the Roman empire, when Christopher Columbus was born—although it fell (as though by some secret logic of history) just before America was discovered. Historically it is closer to us than medieval Mexico; but it feels far away.

All that most of us know about it is that it was beautiful. Its center was one of the loveliest buildings in the entire world, something worthy to rank with the Taj Mahal and Notre Dame: the Cathedral Church of the Holy Wisdom, St. Sophia, with its enormous, airy dome. Some of us also know the strange unforgettable paintings and mosaics of Byzantium: when you enter a Slavic or Greek church today, or look at an icon, what you see is Byzantine art: those tall thoughtful figures, with vast somber eyes. Connoisseurs know also that much of Byzantine art spread through the rest of Europe and the Middle East. So St. Mark's in Venice, St. Basil's cathedral in Moscow, the legendary palace of Harun ar-Raschid in Baghdad—all these are Byzantine. In fact, we are told that it was the beauty of Byzantium which converted the Russians to Christianity. They had been idol-worshipping pagans until the tenth century; but some of their leaders had been baptized; and their monarch Vladimir began to consider which of the great faiths they ought to adopt. He thought of Judaism; but he said, 'No, the Jews are scattered and powerless.' He thought of Mohammedanism; but that is a teetotal religion, and he said, 'To drink is a joy for the Russians, and we cannot live without drinking.' Then he sent envoys to Byzantium. They were taken to see the Christian services at St. Sophia. When they returned, they said, 'We did not know whether we were in heaven or in earth; for on earth elsewhere there is no such splendor. We know that there God dwells among men.' And so the Russians became Christians converted through Byzantium, and to this day their alphabet is the Greek alphabet, and much of their art, their religion, even their way of life, is Byzantine.

We know, too, that it was a complicated and difficult civilization. If we have read Gibbon, we remember how contemptuously he dismissed the Byzantines as a succession of priests and courtiers, and how unwilling he was to pay serious attention to their eager discussions of a God in whom he himself scarcely believed, and to their struggles against the barbarism which he believed had by the eighteenth century been largely exterminated. And if we have glanced into modern histories of Byzantium, we have still been bewildered by painfully complex dynastic disputes, and by almost impenetrably difficult and feverishly excitable arguments over what at first seem to us very tiny religious problems.

And the language of Byzantium is Greek—and not wholly classical Greek, but a special Greek of its own. Few translations of Byzantine Greek works are made, and few scholars study them; if it were not for the Dumbarton Oaks group in Washington, there would hardly be any Byzantine scholarship in the entire American continent. Even apart from the language, the literature is awfully hard: long highly elaborate histories, carefully wrought theological treatises, stiff and formal poems, together with wild folk-romances and epic poetry written in a fantastic blend of cultures and languages.

Perhaps Byzantium is too difficult for us? There might be a sound reason for this. You remember that Spengler said that all important cultures followed the same pattern of growth, maturity, and decay, although at different periods in history. Therefore the people of one culture might well sympathize with the people of another culture, although the two were separated by many centuries, provided they were both at the same stage in their development. For example, he called Mohammed a 'contemporary' of Cromwell. Now, if this is true, you see what follows? It follows that people cannot properly understand a stage of history which is *later in development* than they are—even if it hapened a long time ago. Mohammed could have understood Cromwell perfectly, although Cromwell lived 1000 years after him; but he could not have understood Disraeli, or even Napoleon, because they inhabited a later stage of civilization. (We see this in our daily life: you know how hard it is for a youth of twenty to understand a man of fifty—much harder than it is for a man of fifty to understand a youth.) Well, supposing all that is reasonable and true, then we have not nearly reached the stage of development in our own culture which will correspond to Byzantium, and therefore we cannot understand Byzantium fully—just as we cannot now foresee and understand the world our own great-grandchildren will inhabit.

This may be true. Byzantium has a grown-up, an almost elderly feeling, which we do not possess. As we look at the portraits of men and saintly or divine personages which have survived from Byzantium, and see their great thoughtful eyes, and the long powerful faces in which strength and the ability to feel pain are curiously intermingled, we realize that these people were wise with a wisdom which we have not yet attained; that they knew more about the world's problems, even to understanding that some of those problems cannot be solved. But we do not feel that they are behind us, or inferior to us. The difficulty of understanding them is more like the difficulty that young people have in understanding their elders. We are still young. They are mature, and growing old.

Perhaps that is why so little has been written about Byzantium. There are hardly any novels or plays about it: some failures, of course, but few successes. Offhand, I can recall only Sir Walter Scott's *Count Robert of Paris* and John Masefield's *Basilissa* and *Conquer*. And all these books fail partially, because they are not written with sufficient gusto and richness. The two Masefields deal with the reign of Justinian, but they are supposed to be written by a dry official who has little sympathy with any of the wild passions which blazed through the empire. They are good reporting, but they are like black-and-white reproductions of a complex painting. The Scott novel takes us to Constantinople in the time of the First Crusade. Although it is full of fine ideas, they are not worked out: Scott was very tired when he wrote it. I remember one chapter in which Count Robert is entertained in the sumptuous palace of the emperors. He wakes late, because his wine the night before was drugged. As he wakes, the first thing he sees and hears in the darkness of his room is a tiger, with burning eyes and hungry roaring growls: it had been chained there so that when he moves he will either fall under its claws or else go mad with the effort to avoid it. Now, in his best days, Scott would have made the next half hour into a long splendid combat. But here Count Robert merely throws a stool at the tiger, and fractures its skull, 'which, to say the truth, was none of the largest size'; and then proceeds to escape, with the help of a blind prisoner in the next cell, who has been sawing his way out for years, and of a trained orangoutang which is an assistant warder. A pity that *Count*

Robert of Paris was not written when Scott had more energy: it might have been as good as *Ivanhoe*.

Still, there are some fine non-fiction works about Byzantium. (And here, in Washington, we have one of the few great centers of Byzantine studies: the Dumbarton Oaks Library and Research Collection of Harvard University, which puts out a number of learned studies every few months, and is now established as a source of vital new ideas on the subject.) The standard book is *Byzantium: An Introduction to East Roman Civilization,* edited by Norman Baynes and H. St. L. B. Moss. Mr. Baynes (of the University of London) is really the top scholar on the subject in the English-speaking world, and to make this introduction he has assembled a group of essays by over a dozen specialists, and has added some fine illustrations and a copious bibliography. Byzantine art can be glimpsed in a new and beautiful collection of reproductions of mosaics in Italy: *Byzantine Mosaics,* edited by Peter Meyer.* Very recently the best history of the Byzantine empire was published in this country, written by A. A. Vasiliev. (It was originally planned in Russia before the Revolution; and then—such are the trials and torments of scholarship—it passed through editions in French, Spanish, and Turkish before attaining its present English form.) It is a profoundly scholarly book with a stupendous bibliography; it may be too elaborate for the ordinary reader, but it will become a standard work.

Beginners like myself are more apt to be interested by enthusiastically appreciative studies of those odd and incomprehensible people. Such enthusiasm struck me first in Robert Byron's *The Byzantine Achievement,* a very youthful book issued in London in 1929; and, linked with wisdom, it ap-

---

* There is much of interest also in Steven Runciman's *History of the Crusades,* now appearing from the Cambridge University Press.

pears in one of the most wonderful travel books—no, not travel books—one of the most wonderful books of appreciation, of travel and history, and human character and national psychology, and art and religion, one of the finest books written in our lifetime on apparently one of the least promising subjects, Rebecca West's *Black Lamb and Grey Falcon.*

It describes only one small part of the Byzantine empire, as it is today: the Slavic part of the Balkan peninsula. It penetrates with unexampled sympathy and sensibility into the souls of those strange countries, Serbia, Montenegro, Macedonia, Bosnia, the lands where trouble grows like grass. Beauty and disease, poverty and courage, ignorance and heroism, narrow minds and broad epic spirits, these and many other contrasts are evoked in Miss West's beautiful and eloquent book. (It is written with love—like Browning's poems on Italy; or like a blend of Hemingway's books on Spanish courage and Sitwell's books on Spanish art.) Miss West has a superb style. Consider a sentence or two, which few others could have composed:

> These handsome peasant women bore themselves as if each wore a heavy invisible crown, which meant, I think, an unending burden of responsibility and fatigue.

And this:

> If during the next million generations there is but one human being in every generation who will not cease to inquire into the nature of his fate, even while it strips and bludgeons him, some day we shall read the riddle of the universe.

And this, the reason she wrote the book:

> If a Roman woman had, some years before the sack of Rome, realized why it was going to be sacked, and

what motives inspired the barbarians and what the Romans, and had written down all she knew and felt about it, the record would have been of value to historians. My situation [in 1939-40], though probably not as fatal, is as interesting.

That is our situation at this present time, and it was the situation of the Byzantine empire. We may not be overrun and sacked; but we could be; attempts have been made on us already, and others will be made. When they are, when we resist them and beat them off, we shall realize more of the mystery, the difficulty, and the preciousness of high civilization; and then we shall understand more of the Byzantine achievement. Byzantium is not only in the past. For us it is a possible world of the future. That is part of its power and remoteness. In 1928, W. B. Yeats published a book of poems about his own old age, called *The Tower*. Its first poem, 'Sailing to Byzantium,' distinguishes the temporary animal life of youth and passion, which Yeats saw himself leaving, from the stately permanent life of thought and art. He sees himself as a Christian saint, one of those

> sages standing in God's holy fire
> As in the gold mosaic of a wall . . .

or as a nightingale made by Greek goldsmiths

> Of hammered gold and gold enamelling
> To keep a drowsy emperor awake;
> Or set upon a golden bough to sing
> To lords and ladies of Byzantium
> Of what is past, or passing, or to come.

That is the world of art, and thought, and history which we inhabit when we gaze into the somber eyes of the Byzantine saints, or look at the sumptuous Byzantine buildings. Our own buildings look like *machines à vivre,* made for the present. Theirs seem to be homes of ceremony and prayer, intended to make the mind large enough to contemplate all that

is past, or passing, or to come.

N. Baynes and H. St. L. B. Moss, *Byzantium: An Introduction to East Roman Civilization* (Oxford, 1948).

R. Byron, *The Byzantine Achievement* (Knopf, 1929).

J. Masefield, *Basilissa* (Macmillan, 1940).

J. Masefield, *Conquer* (Macmillan, 1941).

P. Meyer (ed.), *Byzantine Mosaics* (Oxford, 1952).

Sir W. Scott, *Count Robert of Paris.*

A. A. Vasiliev, *History of the Byzantine Empire* (University of Wisconsin Press, 1952).

Rebecca West, *Black Lamb and Grey Falcon* (Viking, 1943).

Books

Unpacking the Great Books

IF you like reading, it is always exciting to unpack a new parcel of books which has just arrived. It is like welcoming guests into your home for the first time. Some of them may be unknown; others you may have met elsewhere; but now, under your own roof, they look different and have a fresh and interesting relation to you.

I have just been welcoming a collection of very distinguished guests indeed, and I am still thinking about them. I have been unpacking two cartons containing the fifty-four volumes which make up the Great Books, and stopping to look into them before putting them on the shelves. They are the series called *Great Books of the Western World,* edited by Robert Hutchins in association with Mortimer Adler. They make a large handsome set, well bound, in a format which looks rather like Mr. Hutchins himself, tall, austere, but attractive.

Before they arrived, I knew what they were intended to be. They are meant to be all, or most of, the permanent books in Western civilization—with one obvious addition, the Bible. There are thousands of books worth reading. There are not so many which are worth reading twice. There are still fewer which are worth reading again and again, and studying with care. Those which are permanently worth reading are the real classics; and this series is meant to contain all, or most, of them.

We know this distinction well enough—although some short-sighted critics and shallow-minded educators have tried to blind our eyes to it. It is the distinction we know so well in music and in art. Thousands of pictures are painted every year. Most of them appear in magazines, and are thrown away. Some of them are bought at exhibitions, and are hung for a while in someone's house. A few of them—only a few—become recognized as masterpieces. Then they enter the noble series of permanent works of art, classics of painting. They join the company of Titian and Rubens and Vermeer and Breughel and Constable. In a way, they become public property, whoever owns them; they even lose their original nationality and become supra-national. They are reproduced all over the Western world, in art books and in postcards and in colored copies; everyone who likes art knows them, and they do not become obsolete with time.

The same applies to music. The Fifth Symphony of Beethoven does not risk becoming out of date. It does not lose its value for us because it was composed 150 years ago by a man who wrote with a quill pen. It is not old. It is not new. It is timeless.

Just in the same way, the great books are timeless. Everyone understands this about the Bible. No one thinks that the Letters of St. Paul have nothing to tell us because they were written 1900 years ago on papyrus in a language now dead. No one studies them chiefly as interesting old documents. The same applies to the Greek and Latin classics: that is why we teach them. If they were simply works which were peculiar because they were so *old,* only antiquarians would care for them. It is because they are timeless that we study them; and it is because they are valuable forever that people take the trouble to learn the difficult languages in which they are written. Long after the English language has ceased to be spoken, if there is any kind of civilization worth living in, there will be professors who will teach English so that their pupils can learn to read Shakespeare. No doubt they will be thought of as eccentrics for teaching a dead language; but they will be right.

That is the principle on which the *Great Books of the Western World* were selected and published; and I was moved and rather excited when the cartons arrived and I began unpacking them.

The first thing that came out was two volumes containing the whole of Shakespeare's plays. I looked in, to find with regret that they were printed in double column. No doubt it saves paper, but it is ugly and hard to read. Yet as soon as my eyes fell on the open page, the old delight swept me away: it was Clarence's dream from *Richard III:*

> Then came wandering by
> A shadow like an angel, with bright hair
> Dabbled in blood, and he shrieked out aloud,
> 'Clarence is come, false, fleeting, perjured Clarence,
> That stabbed me in the field by Tewkesbury.
> Seize on him, Furies, take him unto torment.'

With that, methought, a legion of foul fiends
Environed me, and howled in mine ears
Such hideous cries, that, with the very noise,
I trembling waked, and, for a season after,
Could not believe but that I was in hell,
Such terrible impression made my dream.

With love and reluctance I shelved these two books—for the essence of a real classic is that, once you know it, you begin to love it, and, once you love it, it seems constantly new to you.

The next volume was a surprise. It was a collection of the treatises of Greek mathematicians. I opened it too. My eye fell on this sentence:

Every segment bounded by a parabola and a chord Qq is equal to four-thirds of the triangle which has the same base as the segment and equal height.

Hastily, I closed that volume and shelved it, and reached for another. This was Goethe's strange imaginative drama, *Faust*. I can read it in German, but this was of course in English, and the first thing to look at was the translation. It is, I am glad to say, a good vigorous version by George Madison Priest of Princeton, and it looks fine, printed in big single column. Again I read a few lines, and again the magic of well-known poetry came over me.

But the next volume was half of Gibbon's *Decline and Fall of the Roman Empire*. This was a puzzle. Why had the editors chosen this? It is not very well written: at least, most readers now grow tired of its monumental dignity and find its style painfully monotonous. And it is very inadequate as history. It might have been better if they had printed the revision of it by the modern historian J. B. Bury, which corrects many of the misstatements and fills in some of the gaps;

but this was a reprint of the *Everyman* edition, which is really obsolete. A puzzle.

After this came out another volume of science, modern science this time. I opened it at Faraday's lectures on electricity, and met this inspiring sentence:

> Spermaceti is a better conductor than shellac.

Reflecting that it would take me time, perhaps more time than I have left, to learn to love that as well as I love Shakespeare, I shelved Faraday.

The next to emerge were two volumes of St. Thomas Aquinas. These were much more carefully edited and annotated than the others, doubtless because Mr. Adler himself thinks highly of St. Thomas. I opened them, too. At once, at the first half-page, I was aware of being in the presence of a really powerful mind. Logic, when used cleanly and boldly, is always impressive, like a good surgical operation; and it is impossible to read St. Thomas without feeling that his mind was one of the most brilliant cutting instruments ever produced.

Thereafter I picked out one of the two volumes of the *Syntopicon*. This is a remarkable job. It is a collection of about 100 essays by Mr. Adler on the great ideas which are constantly discussed in the *Great Books*—and therefore by the wisest of mankind. We cannot think out every problem for ourselves, without guidance. Problems such as the nature of the state, the essence of marriage, the meaning of punishment would occupy a trained philosopher for many years. What Mr. Adler does is to give us the guidance by showing us the main aspects of each of these problems as they occur in the *Great Books,* by bringing the discussion together, and by adding a host of references to the *Great Books* and to many other works which touch on the same themes. From one of these essays, and from careful study of the passages referred to, we can start to reason for ourselves. And it is impossible to think over many big problems without growing bigger mentally; most people with narrow minds either concentrate on one problem or deal habitually in trivialities.

Following this, there came up Number One in the series. This is Mr. Hutchins' introduction to the entire project. Its core is a short essay in which he justifies the idea and traverses some of the objections to it. (One obvious one: why not some of the great books of the East as well?) I wish I could say that I thought this was a satisfactory introduction. Stimulating it is, as everything Mr. Hutchins writes is stimulating. But it is also rather arrogant, when it ought to be persuasive; it is chilly, when, among all these monuments of wisdom, we need warmth; and it is sometimes mistaken. For example, Mr. Hutchins has an enormous contempt for American education—a contempt which he does not try to conceal and which sometimes misleads him. Listen:

> If you are an American under the age of 90, you can have acquired . . . only the faintest glimmerings of the beginnings of liberal education . . . Ask yourself whether you mastered the liberal arts. I am willing to wager that, if you read any great books at all [at college], you read very few, that you read one without reference to the others, and that for the most part you read only excerpts from them.

Well, this might be true for some colleges, and for some groups; but Mr. Hutchins would lose his wager to several thousand graduates of Columbia College in New York, who have been reading Great Books, whole, and together, and purposefully, for the last 15 years, as a regular part of their undergraduate education. He would lose to graduates of other colleges, and even to alumni of some Eastern schools. But apart from the inaccuracy, don't you think the tone is rather unfortunate? Americans do not usually respond well to a tone of pitying contempt, and surely the implication that we have all been badly educated and don't know it is both pitying and contemptuous. There are several ways to convince people that they ought to raise their standards in literature and in music and in art; but this method is usually the least successful—even when, as here, it is based on profound conviction. I say this with some emphasis, because I am devoted to the ideal which the *Great Books* represent, and I think it is very unfortunate that many potential readers will be made indifferent, or even hostile, by Mr. Hutchins' introduction.

At last, I shelved the entire series and sat back to look them over. Fifty-four volumes. Seventy-two authors, more or less. (Some are groups.) About one-third of them came from the eighteenth and nineteenth centuries; about one-third from the Renaissance and the Middle Ages; about one-third from the civilization of Greece and Rome. Fair enough. The three high levels of our culture.

There are very few commentaries. Only the books. There are brief biographical notes about each author (which I found too difficult for the average reader). I believe that one more volume like the *Syntopicon* should have been added, simply to tell readers what the books are and in what pattern they were written—to explain, for instance, that *Paradise Lost* was meant to become an English and Christian Homer and Vergil; that *Gulliver's Travels* was a parody of the contemporary travel tale in the tradition of satire; and so on.

The translations—on the whole, they are good; but awfully pedestrian. Homer in prose; Lucretius in prose; Dante in prose; one Greek tragedian in verse (and what verse!), the other two in prose. We lose a great deal here, and a companion volume dealing with the aesthetic form of the books could have told us how much we lose.

But the strangest thing about the *Great Books* is this. Most of them are distinguished works of history or philosophy or fiction. But some are scientific books, which few people read for pleasure, and very few even for instruction. Now, the method of science is a splendid human achievement, and one of the bases of human life. We all respect it; we ought all to understand it. But the books produced by scientists of 200 or 2,000 years ago are not *permanent* in the same way as the books of great poets or philosophers. The surgical techniques of Hippocrates, the astronomical concepts of Ptolemy, have been superseded, or *absorbed* into later work. The psalms of David, the metaphysics of Aristotle, have not been, and will never be.

And as soon as we realize this, we begin to observe omissions which are quite as inexplicable. Why did the editors omit nearly all the great books about the law? It is wonderful to see man, by the use of simple reason, building up a code of behavior, which is more or less permanent, which is far above local custom or the will of a single ruler, and which continues to produce first-rate minds—such as that of Mr. Hutchins himself. And why is there no oratory—which is a powerful force in religion and politics, and which often carries powerful ideas powerfully expressed? Then again, we notice that Marx is included as the author of a Great Book, without much emphasis on his many confusions and mistakes. Now, why? Because he has affected the minds of many men? In that case, surely we ought also to have the works of the Protestant reformers, such as Luther and Calvin, who initiated and explained a bigger and a deeper revolution.

And why should we have so many second-rate English books, and omit so many first-rate non-English books? Is Sterne's *Tristram Shandy* really worth anything, compared with Molière, who is omitted—or even compared with Voltaire's *Candide*? Is Boswell's *Life of Johnson* worth an entire volume in a series described as representing Western Civilization, when we get nothing of Saint-Simon, who was a better writer with a far more important subject?

As I sat and looked at the shelves, I thought over all these things. I was happy to have the books. I admired the breadth of the plan, and the excellence of its physical execution. I looked forward to reading some of the great books, like Pascal's *Provincial Letters,* which I had never studied. But I regretted the arbitrariness and occasional freakishness of the selection; I wished that at least one-third of the volumes had been replaced by other, greater books; and I thought that too little encouragement was given to their readers. Education is difficult: particularly self-education. We should try not to make it seem impossible.

———

Great Books of the Western World, edited by Robert Hutchins in association with Mortimer Adler (The Encyclopaedia Britannica in association with the University of Chicago, 1952).

Science for the Unscientific

————————————

Hᴏᴡ many fine subjects there are on which nobody ever writes books! . . . or hardly anybody! . . . Mountains, climate, magic, birth and death, comedy—there are scarcely a dozen books worth reading on these, and on many other, grand themes. (No doubt the central reason for this is that, as soon as one begins to get inside a subject, one has no desire to write about it: experience is nearly always superior to recording and description. Then again, as long as one is finding out more and more every week about a topic, one dares not stop and set down what one imagines to be firmly established. It is not quite true. It isn't complete . . .)

Now, critics are supposed sometimes to sink under the weight of current books: to complain that too many are being published. I cannot agree with that. Of course I see a lot of repetitious books, and a lot of inadequate books. But even then I think that some of them have to be published simply to serve a public which did not read earlier works on the same subjects, while others are meant to awaken public interest in a theme which might seem repulsive if treated in full. Apart from those, I have the delight of reading a large number of good books on difficult and important subjects: good books old and new.

Yet, in between them all, I am conscious of huge gaps, interstices of ignorance, which should be bridged by books, but are not—or, at best, are crossed only by slender ropes of essays, or a light network of airy debate, slightly fastened together by flimsy commonplaces applied at the last moment by an optimistic editor.

One of the largest of these gaps is surely Science. The scientists have lots of books, of course, within their own world; but they do not often write books for the unscientific, and when they do they sometimes fail to make their subject pleasing or interesting. Someone once told me that Paul de Kruif was disdained by pure scientists because he had written successful books of what is called 'vulgarization.' If so, they are unwise. He has done them a great service. (Here I speak with a certain emphasis, for my own subject, the classics, was very nearly killed by specialists who despised the public and would not explain their own work.)

Immanuel Kant said that the two greatest objects in existence were 'the starry sky above, the moral law within.' And surely the most wonderful physical thing that exists is the macrocosm: the stellar universe. Living in cities, we see the stars too seldom; and those who live in the country usually go to bed too early; so that only scientists and lovers and an occasional poet can look at the grandest spectacle of the universe.

On this splendid theme, the best book I have read for a

long time is Fred Hoyle's *The Nature of the Universe*. It is a set of lectures given over the British radio by a Cambridge scientist who was still in his twenties—which means young enough to be bold and fresh enough to be vivid. No doubt the specialists will tell us that some of his descriptions of the universe are oversimplified. Still, they are clear. Sometimes they are eloquent. And they seem to be fair enough, for when he is describing a theory he usually tells you it *is* a theory and not an established system of facts. Hoyle is in the direct line of succession to Rutherford and Jeans. Sir James Jeans made his biggest impact on the world with a book called *The Universe Around Us* (which for many people now alive was the first introduction to modern astronomy and physics), while Rutherford held that no discovery of his was complete until he had put it into easily understandable English.

As well as being clear, Hoyle's book is poetic. Astronomy is one of the sciences which often verge into poetry—indeed, even the names of some of the inhabitants of the cosmos are evocative: red giants, white dwarfs, and Magellanic clouds . . . The most poetic thing in the book is of course imagination, not observation: it is his conception of the process he calls *continuous creation*. The idea is that the whole cosmos is full of the thinly scattered raw material of nebulae and solar systems and universes, and that—like clouds gathering above a summer sea, or like thoughts collecting within the mind—groups of this material slowly and gradually grow together, millions of years ago, yesterday, today, tomorrow, millions of years in the future, making separate universes, each of which coalesces and solidifies and comes into shape and then (after living for its time) passes out of our ken into dimensions where we can no longer perceive it, scarcely even conceive its mode of existence.

A much longer and more thorough book on astronomy for the layman has been written by J. B. Sidgwick and edited by W. K. Green. This is *The Heavens Above*. It is far more densely packed with information than Hoyle's work; but most of it is meant for a mind unlike mine. I belong to the group which stops long before calculus, and which cannot use a slide rule. The other group . . . when playing bridge, the other group lays down eight cards and says, 'The rest are ours'; and they honestly do not believe me when I want to see the hand played out and fail to understand why it was obvious all the time. So Mr. Sidgwick assumes that his readers can carry out complicated calculations with enjoyment: quite soon he is explaining the difference between sidereal and synodic periods, and substituting functions in the equation $\alpha + \beta = \theta$, and canceling out common factors. Good; but not for me.

Apparently there are at least three different kinds of science books for the layman. The first type is the manual, rather dry but full of information: such is *The Heavens Above*. The second type is a collection of lectures, which strive to interest, and do not pretend to completeness. Such is Hoyle's book. Although lectures cannot be complete, they must be integrated. I have recently read two books of this kind, one of which stuck together while the other fell into pieces. The failure was *The Physical Basis of Mind*—a collection of BBC talks: since they were given by ten different people and scarcely co-ordinated at all, the net result was almost nil.

A more coherent job is *Doubt and Certainty in Science,* by J. Z. Young, a single series of BBC lectures. The title is not much good, for the book does not deal with the philosophical problem of knowledge versus opinion in science generally; and I don't think the announced purpose of the book is fulfilled: for Mr. Young sets out to discuss 'how the brain makes communication between human beings possible,' which ought to have led him into examinations of language, gesture, and the social organization of beings such as ants, birds, fish, bees, and the many herd-animals of which we are one species. Still he gives us a stimulating introduction to the relation between the brain, the body, the nervous system, and the processes of thought, emotion, action. And the entire book is pervaded by the indispensable sense of Wonder. King Philip II of Spain is reported to have said that if he had been consulted at the time of the Creation, he could have saved the Almighty from making some unnecessary blunders. This is the spirit which a scientist should avoid at all costs; and Mr. Young shows us clearly that the more one discovers about the structure of the body—or indeed of any part of the universe—the *less* certain one can be that one has grasped the scheme of things entire.

Well, these are two types of science book. There is a third type: evocative description, often moving into narrative. Naturally it is difficult to write this kind of book about the inorganic sciences, although I sometimes wish some talented author would take us into the minds of great mathematicians or physicists and show us, stage by stage, how they reached their conclusions. (Why is there only one even passable book on Sir Isaac Newton?) This kind of book has been brought to the fore recently by the success of Rachel Carson's *The Sea Around Us*. Her earlier work, *Under the Sea-Wind,* has now been reissued. The former was about the sea. This is about the shore—not, as you and I see it, the frontier of the land beyond which stretches the 'salt, unplumbed, estranging sea,' but rather the edge of the populous deeps, the holiday and honeymoon spot which the inhabitants of the ocean visit from time to time, where they meet with the birds and the men who make their living from the waters, where they are sometimes born and sometimes brought to maturity, and to which they return years later. The book is thinner than *The*

Sea Around Us—as is natural, since it plies through shallower waters; and, for my taste, it suffers from the old Ernest Thompson Seton habit of personifying individual animals, Anguilla the Eel, and so forth—whereas what matters about eels is that they come in multitudes, and are best described as a crowd, not as a singleton. However, it is full of intimate knowledge and genuine love of that strange, often unlovable, almost incomprehensible world from which we came, the world of the water.

American and British writers do this kind of book rather well. When well done, it usually lasts. We can keep it on our shelves to solace us—in the winter, when we cannot walk in the woods; in the spring, when we are overworked and forgetful; always, to tell us about other lands which we can never fully know. Let me here praise a trilogy by Ivan Sanderson, called *Animal Treasure, Caribbean Treasure,* and *Living Treasure*—published in 1937, 1939, and 1941 with humorous and charming illustrations by the author, who is a skilled naturalist, explorer, and artist. I read them again at least once a year. The last time I opened them I was in bed with a virus; but soon I found myself, together with Sanderson, in the following predicaments:

> surrounded by a large gang of baboons on a lonely trail in West Africa, at dusk . . . (it does no good to stone them, for they stone you back; but you get out of it by laughing and screaming and acting crazy) . . .

> penetrating the vast cave of bats and devil-birds in Mount Aripo in Trinidad, through a 'screeching pandemonium' which Sanderson himself says is rather like Doré's hell . . .

> aloft 50 feet high among the branches of a dead tree which has been secretly and inwardly burning for half

an hour, and is just beginning to roar and send up 'a jet of nearly liquid heat' . . .

A few of these adventures will make anyone forget a virus. Let me also recall another book like this which I read and enjoyed, and then, alas, lent to somebody: *One Day on Beetle Rock*, by Sally Carrighar, published by Knopf some years ago.

And finally, let me recommend a book written by a man who is not really a scientist or a trained naturalist, but rather a cosmopolitan and a city dweller—yet he has come to hate heavy buildings and crowds of people, and to realize that, if we want to live well, we must live in touch with nature. This is Joseph Wood Krutch's *Desert Year*, finely illustrated by Rudolf Freund. A few months ago I was walking along the edge of the Grand Canyon, looking at that wild world. Along the trail on the rim, the Forestry Service had placed discreet little labels explaining the trees and the wild life. These were wisely interspersed with paragraphs to think over, thoughts in the manner of Thoreau on the proper relation of man to nature. It was delightful there, with the evening colors falling on the crumbling temples of the Canyon floor and the birds hawking about in the sea of air below my feet, to meet a quiet, sane sentence from Krutch's earlier book, *The Twelve Seasons*, and to see that, in those surroundings where falsity is impossible and affectation is unbearable, they sounded true. Good science books tell us the truth about bigger things than ourselves.

The Physical Basis of Mind (Blackwell, Oxford, 1950).
S. Carrighar, *One Day on Beetle Rock* (Knopf, 1944).
R. Carson, *The Sea Around Us* (Oxford, 1951).

R. Carson, *Under the Sea-Wind* (Oxford, 1952).

F. Hoyle, *The Nature of the Universe* (Harper, 1950).

J. W. Krutch, *The Desert Year* (Sloane, 1952).

J. W. Krutch, *The Twelve Seasons* (Sloane, 1949).

L. T. More, *Isaac Newton* (Scribner, 1934).

I. Sanderson, *Animal Treasure* (Viking, 1937).

I. Sanderson, *Caribbean Treasure* (Viking, 1939).

I. Sanderson, *Living Treasure* (Viking, 1941).

J. B. Sidgwick, *The Heavens Above* (American ed. by W. K. Green, Oxford, 1950).

J. Z. Young, *Doubt and Certainty in Science* (Oxford, 1951).

The Historian's Job

———————————

THE historian's job is to tell us about the past. If you think about it for a moment, that really is an astonishing notion. We are often informed how remarkable it is that an astronomer is able to describe the constitution and motions of a star on the other side of the universe, or that a physicist can explain the behavior of tiny entities which are too small to see (even through a microscope) and yet too complicated to diagrammatize. But it is almost equally strange that a man writing a book in 1953 should be able to tell us about the actions, the appearance, the very thoughts of scores of people whom he never saw, living and working in a world which has long since disappeared. Some historians have—after laboring long at the task—concluded that it was almost impossible to achieve. There is a fine passage from Froude, describing the end of the Middle Ages:

> The paths trodden by the footsteps of ages were broken up: old things were passing away, and the faith and the life of ten centuries were dissolving like a dream. Chivalry was dying; the abbey and the castle were soon together to crumble into ruins; and all the forms, desires, beliefs, convictions of the old world were passing away, never to return . . . And now it is all gone—like an unsubstantial pageant faded; and between us and the old English there lies a gulf of mystery which the prose of the historian will never adequately bridge. They cannot come to us, and our imagination can but feebly penetrate to them. Only among the aisles of the cathedral, only as we gaze upon their silent figures sleeping on their tombs, some faint conceptions float before us of what these men were when they were alive; and perhaps in the sound of church-bells, that peculiar creation of medieval age, which falls upon the ear like an echo of a vanished world.*

Handsome prose, isn't it? And filled with the right emotions for the historian: nostalgia, imagination, and humility. There is a fine thirteenth-century Spanish tomb in the Cloisters, the tomb of the Count of Urgel, which I often look at with the same feelings of wonder and distance.

The historian's job is difficult, then, but not impossible. There are at least three different ways of doing it. We can easily be disappointed if we overlook this and expect all historians to follow the same plan.

The first type is not, strictly speaking, a professional historian's work at all; but it is history none the less. This is a

---

* J. A. Froude, *History of England,* Chapter I.

collection of materials, memories of interesting events set down by an eyewitness. Such a book never tells the whole story, because its author does not care about the whole story and does not know enough to relate it. And it does not usually interpret events by fitting them into a large pattern of social, economic, and political change. But it is nearly always an invaluable collection of facts which all other historians must take into account (or else show good reason for disbelieving); it bridges the gulf between the present and the past, by speaking of things really seen and experienced; and it usually has the brisk variety and unexpectedness of life. A famous example of this type is *The Acts of the Apostles,* which was either written by a man who had shared in the experiences described, or else based on his memoirs. There are two other such books, which have long been cordially hated and hopelessly misunderstood. These are the two sets of 'Memoirs' by Julius Caesar—sometimes wrongly called his *Commentaries.* They are cool, dry, apparently factual accounts of the war in France in which Caesar trained his private army, and of the civil war in which he attacked and overthrew the constitutional government of his country. I say 'apparently factual' because he himself deliberately chose to write them not as history, in the highly developed sense which the Greeks and Romans knew, but as objective notes ostensibly intended for future historians to use and to believe. They are about as honest and well balanced as *Mein Kampf*; but the skill with which they are composed has led some historians to accept them as the plain statement of unadulterated facts.

Still, there are few writers of this kind of history who have much adroitness in disguising reality. Most of them do tell something like the truth as they saw it, although they do not attempt to tell the whole truth. Two of my favorite autobiographies fall into this class. One is the life story of William Cobbett, the tough, bluff Englishman who lived in the United

States from 1792 to 1800 and made the country too hot to hold him by issuing torrid anti-revolutionary propaganda; returned to Britain and was soon tossed into prison for denouncing the abuse of discipline in the army; ran a first-rate popular newspaper; sat in Parliament; and loved his country with a warm physical love and deep knowledge. The other is the autobiography of Dr. Benjamin Franklin, filled with his peculiar blend of ingenuity and ingenuousness, which makes it easy to see why President Jefferson called him 'the most agreeable man in company that he had ever known.'

Two charming collections of such memories, recently published, are well worth reading. One of them is *The Memoirs of a Monticello Slave*—the reminiscences of Isaac, one of Mr. Jefferson's slaves, who dictated to an interviewer all that he remembered, just over a century ago. The other is *The Letters of Private Wheeler,* a regular soldier who served under Wellington and wrote a splendid series of letters home about his adventures. The beauty of such books is that, while we read them, we seem actually to hear the voice of a man who knew Mr. Jefferson, of a soldier who marched up to the terrible walls of Badajoz and fought for three days at Waterloo. The past speaks through them.

The second type of history book is a reconstruction. This is an attempt to re-create the past from a few facts, and usually from inadequate facts. It is hard to do this. To succeed, the historian must carefully combine isolated data so that they support and explain one another; interpret documents which were written with no thought of aiding him; often combine the talents of a lawyer, an art critic, an anthropologist, and a psychoanalyst; and always be prepared to admit that he does not know, and is only inferring. Much of the history of the distant past has to be reconstructed in this manner.

If both the writer and the reader will fairly admit that

certain knowledge cannot usually be attained, then such works are delightful and valuable. In his presidential address to the American Historical Association in December 1951, Professor Robert Schuyler praised the historian Maitland for just this virtue. Haziness, he said, was recognized by Maitland for what it was. It was allowed to remain hazy. It was not 'given the semblance of clarity by having an unhistorical and false lucidity forced upon it.'

There is a fine example of this in *The Oxford History of England*. This majestic series of fourteen volumes is not yet complete, but ten are now out, and they are indispensable works. In Volume 1, the late R. G. Collingwood, that brilliant man who was both a historian and an archaeologist and (unlikely combination!) a philosopher, applies his mind to the legend of King Arthur. Who was Arthur? Who were his knights? Fables? Myths? Retrojections of medieval men into the late Roman empire? Collingwood takes the stories as we have them in the earliest form: King Arthur was recorded, by men who lived not many generations after his death, to have fought the pagan invaders of Roman Britain. He had an odd title, *dux bellorum,* leader in the wars. He fought all over Britain. He had knights in armor. He was finally killed by one of his own men. Not much more is recorded. But out of this Collingwood constructs the admirable inference that Arthur was in fact a gifted Roman-British professional soldier, who led a force organized to meet the recurrent barbarian invasions—namely, a mobile unit of heavy cavalry, with men, and perhaps horses too, armored so that even when outnumbered they could still rout a horde of savages, poorly organized and lightly equipped. He was not a territorial ruler, but was apparently employed by the various Christian chiefs of different areas of Britain—hence his adventures far and near. And he was the last hope of the

Celtic people of Britain, so that when he was killed (Collingwood suggests that the Mordred story means there was dissension within the ranks of his own small force) they would not believe he was really dead, but spoke of him as still alive, waiting his time to return and champion their cause once again.

This is not all the story, of course. Professor Roger Loomis and other scholars have shown how Arthur and his men also gathered much of their strength and magic from the pre-Christian stories of Celtic gods, and from a religion which, although the Christian missionaries drove it out, still lingered in the recesses of men's minds and in that strange region where poetry is born. And tomorrow a British plowman might quite well turn up a stone, with an inscription on it, which would disprove Collingwood's reconstruction of the basic story of the human Arthur. But if that possibility is acknowledged, as it is in the *Oxford History,* then we can accept the story and, by using it, understand a little more about that grim time when the empire was falling and even Christianity seemed in danger, as it often has seemed to be since then.

There is a third kind of history book, which is not so much a reconstruction as a selection and a compression. Here there are plenty of facts, lots of records, dispatches and deeds, private letters and public announcements, maps, and even photographs. The historian has to choose those which will make the story clear; arrange them so as to bring out the essentials of historical change; and then, with such gifts of style and imagination as he possesses, convert them into something less like a scientific statement than a work of art. The professional scholars distrust this kind of writing; but when it is proved trustworthy they usually acknowledge that it is the crown of their profession. Life is sometimes exciting; and this type of history can convey the excitement. Life contains nobility and beauty; such histories will evoke the beauty and reflect the nobility. Life is frequently very funny: the right historian can make us laugh. For instance, take John Miller's history of the War of Independence, called *Triumph of Freedom,* and turn to his account of the Battle of Trenton. We knew that Washington crossed the Delaware among floating blocks of ice on a bitter Christmas night, and attacked the Hessian troops on 26 December 1776. But the Hessians had been doing some serious Christmas drinking, and their colonel, Rahl, had to be awakened by his orderly to confront the double perils of Washington's artillery and a terrific hangover. The strategic surprise conducted by Washington was complete. After less than an hour's fighting, the Hessians surrendered; and, Mr. Miller tells us,

> Among the slain was Colonel Rahl. He died as he had lived—brave and drunk.

I can recommend Mr. Miller's book heartily. And just as heartily let me recommend a splendid trilogy by Arthur Bryant, dealing with the Napoleonic era. They are called *Years of Endurance* (1793-1802), *Years of Victory* (1802-1812), and *The Age of Elegance* (1812-1822). They began to appear at just the right moment, when the British were standing alone against Hitler and when the entire continent of Europe appeared to be united under a single master who was forging it into a weapon with which to destroy or enslave Great Britain—just as it had appeared under the Emperor Napoleon. It is one of the highest uses of history, to remind individuals and nations that greatness is always possible; and I believe that Bryant's books had that effect. But apart from their patriotism, they are full of general interest and charm. Battles, as we know, are terribly hard to describe. Stendhal thought no soldier had much chance of understanding what went on in them; and Tolstoy believed that not even the generals knew. But as we read Bryant's descriptions of great battles we know very well that the generals on both sides (and many of the experienced officers) in the Napoleonic wars were fully aware of everything essential that was happening; and yet Bryant manages to give us the enlisted man's point of view, too, and reports how he drank or swore; and he tells us how the young officers joked and capered even in the toughest spots. There is an entire chapter of nearly forty pages on Waterloo, and I cannot read it without wild excitement.

History is more than battles. And so Bryant shows us what England, France, Spain, and Portugal actually looked like: how their people fed, and worked, and amused themselves: he makes them live. To describe London in 1814, he uses an admirable device. He shows us the Czar of Russia (who had come to England for the peace celebration) riding round the city early in the morning, followed by his Cossack attendants with long lances and sheepskin cloaks; and he tells us what the Czar saw. It is like a fine set of Rowlandson drawings, with something grander in it, that Rowlandson never saw:

> the tottering old taverns and warehouses of Scotland Yard, the gardens of Northumberland House, the conical water tower of York Buildings, Somerset House rising like a Venetian palace from the water, and Paul's dome floating above the houses and spires. And binding Westminster to the city, the city to the world, and man to the ages, the great stream flowed seawards, green and grey . . .

Well, these are the three types of history: the memories, which give individual experience; the reconstructions, which apply logic to scanty records; and the imaginative descriptions, which, from the endless flow of facts and events spawned in millions by the tireless human race, selects those which are truly important and gives us not only their casual connections, but something of the rich emotion and imagination which accompanied them when they occurred, and without which the past is truly dead. It is a noble task, to keep it alive.

———

A. Bryant, *The Years of Endurance* (*1793-1802*) (Harper, 1942).

A. Bryant, *Years of Victory* (*1802-1812*) (Harper, 1945).

A. Bryant, *The Age of Elegance* (*1812-1822*) (Harper, 1951).

W. Cobbett, *Life, Written by Himself* (World's Classics, 1924).

B. Franklin, *Autobiography* (Modern Library, 1939).

J. Miller, *Triumph of Freedom* (Little Brown, 1948).

The Oxford History of England (Oxford, 1931—).

Wheeler, *The Letters of Private Wheeler* (ed. B. H. Liddell Hart, Houghton Mifflin, 1952).

Isaac, *The Memoirs of a Monticello Slave* (ed. R. Logan, The University of Virginia, 1952).

The Making of Literature

IT is a pleasure to read good books and to talk about them. But there is another pleasure connected with books, which is less often enjoyed and more difficult to secure. This is the pleasure of learning how the books we love were made. Where on earth—or where in heaven—did Shakespeare get the idea for *A Midsummer-Night's Dream*, blending Greek myths with British fairy lore? How did Eliot conceive *The Waste Land*, and how did he work it out? Is it complete as it stands, or merely a series of fragments, or perhaps a heavily cut edition of the lost original? Why did Tolstoy write *War and Peace* seven times, and make his wife copy it out seven times? What was he doing to it? adding material? rearranging the incidents and descriptions already there? or smoothing and harmonizing the style? It is hard to think of Count

Leo Nikolayevich rolling on the rug in an agonized search for the right word, like Flaubert; but he was surely searching for something, and he surely found it. What was it?

It is an enthralling question to ask about any book, any poem, any piece of art—in fact, about any work of the mind. *How was it made?*

And it is not a trivial or superficial question. It helps us to understand the work itself. I have always admired the George Washington Bridge over the Hudson between Manhattan and New Jersey. It is a noble span. Its rhythm harmonizes with the majestic sweep of the river, and the pillars at its entry stand as proudly as the Palisades. On a bright morning the cars glitter in the sunlight as they rush across it, so that it looks like a straight and rapid stream of light in the air, crossing the more darkly gleaming water far below. If you walk across it, you will feel that it is not a dead mass of stone and metal, but a living thing, quivering and humming like a great ship at sea. A splendid piece of architecture—and yet I confess I have admired it more since I learned that the architects changed their original plan. They meant to make the pylons at each end solid columns of concrete. But when they had put up the mighty steel framework, they looked at it, and decided that the pure metal, with the sky shining through it, was far more noble and beautiful. They were right. And, by knowing that fact about the making of the bridge, I have learned to appreciate it more, as a work of art.

In the same way we can very often enjoy a book more if we understand more about the process of its conception and delivery, and about its author's life and work. When we do, we nearly always find our respect for it increased. We see there is more in it than we had divined. We admire the author more, for his singular character, his complex experience, his skillful technique, and even his sheer tenacity. We usually realize that even the simplest poem is the product of much more work than we imagine, passing through the minds of many men before it meets its final author; and that most artists, thinkers, and creators lead a life far more difficult than that of the ordinary man and woman. We pity them, instead of blaming them, for their failures; and we exalt them all the more for their unique successes.

Recently I have been reading three books which deal with this question on different levels.

The first is *The Notebooks of Henry James,* edited by two Harvard professors, the late F. O. Matthiessen and K. B. Murdock. This is a big work of some 400 tall pages. It is a transcript of nine manuscript books in which Henry James kept ideas for plays and novels, lists of odd and interesting names, personal impressions, character sketches, and spiritual affirmations, over a period of thirty-three years from 1878 to 1911. There are also several long scenarios and sketches for novels, which complete the picture of a hard-working, earnest craftsman, devoted to his job.

I must admit that I do not admire Henry James's novels very much. Their style bothers me, as it has bothered many another—not so much because it is involved, but because it seems to me to lack the glitter and brilliance and charm of the society it pictures. When Proust describes an evening party in fashionable society, his sentences curve as gracefully as the hostess's satin train, they are full of jewels (both real and paste), iridescent with aigrettes, and fans, and perfume. But when James does a party, it seems to be full of complicated intrigues and difficult relationships, but lacking the color and gallantry which surrounded them and made them both more difficult and more exciting. And I must say also that he seems to me to have been unlucky in his choice of subject. One of his main themes, for instance, is immensely important—the relation between young America and old Europe; but he usually treats it only in what has proved to be its least important manifestation, the association of rich, purposeless, rootless American travelers with *le high-life* in Europe, and vice versa.

However, that is no doubt a blind spot in me. Every reader has his blind spots. And certainly the reading of James's *Notebooks* has done something to remove this one.

Among other things, they show that he was mainly concerned with *one* world—not the world of thought, nor the world of politics, nor the world of religion, and scarcely the world of fine art and music, but the world of social and family relationships. He gave up much of his life to that world. Sometimes he felt it was an interference with his work. Here is his entry for 11 November 1882, when he was nearly forty:

> Thanks to 'society,' which, in the shape of various surviving remnants of the season, and a succession of transient Americans, and several country visits, continued to mark me for its own during the greater part of the month of August, I had not even time to finish that last sentence [in his notebooks] written more than three months ago . . . My record of work for the whole past year is terribly small . . .

But more often he realized that society was the source of his work. Much of the conversation at those interminable Victorian and Edwardian dinner parties appears to have been high-level gossip, anecdotes about the family troubles of other members of society. James wrote many of these stories down. He used some of them as plots for his books, and others he recorded for future use in his notebooks. For instance, Mrs. Anstruther-Thompson, sitting next to him at Lady Lindsay's told him a shocking tale of family jealousy and revenge.

A Scottish laird died. His son became his heir, and inherited the big house full of fine pictures and furniture. The mother survived, and went on living in the house. But the young man married, so that his mother had to move out into a small dower-house elsewhere. She took with her some of the family treasures. The son asked to have them returned. The mother refused. The quarrel grew hot, and finally developed into a lawsuit. And in court the mother—in order to win the case, or at least to beat her son and her enemy—solemnly declared that she had been an adulteress and that the boy was illegitimate.

It is a fine story. James wrote it down as soon as he heard it, and thought over it again and again. At last, four years later, it grew into his novel, *The Spoils of Poynton*. There are many more such stories in the *Notebooks*. It will surprise most of us to learn that James's famous tale of demoniac possession, 'The Turn of the Screw,' was told to him by the Archbishop of Canterbury, who had himself heard it from a rather vague lady. And there is one story which really haunts me. You know Maupassant's 'The Necklace,' in which a woman borrows a string of pearls, or diamonds, loses them, and impoverishes her husband and herself over many years in order to pay back their value—only to find that they were paste? Well, James took this idea and reversed it. A woman (in his story) who has given up a stage career to marry a clergyman leaves, at her death, a lot of junk jewelry, among which there is one necklace of *real* pearls. Where did she get them? That is the basic plot. James published it, as 'Paste,' in 1899. But haven't we seen it more recently, and more vividly, revived, as 'Mr. Knowall,' by Somerset Maugham, in his group of short filmed stories, *Quartet*? There the woman is not dead, but alive. The pearls are around her neck. Her husbands bets that they are false. A jewel expert takes the bet, looks at them, and sees that they are real, worth a small fortune. What does he do? . . . It is a fine story.

You see how, in talking about one author's attitude to his work, we move on naturally to others. I have been reading another book which describes the techniques of creative writing used by twenty or thirty poets, and which reveals a great deal by comparing and contrasting them. This is *Poems in Process,* by Phyllis Bartlett. It is a shorter volume than the James *Notebooks,* but it covers a fair amount of ground. Its purpose is to give 'an account of how poets have actually written their verses'—but in fact it confines the account to English and American poets, and does not include all the greatest names. (There is nothing, for instance, on the variations in Shakespeare's text which appear to have come from his own hand and mind.) I should have liked to learn more about French and Italian and German and Spanish poets; and a book—no, two books—could be written on the methods used by the Greek and Latin poets, who were skilled technicians. However, we are grateful for what Miss Bartlett has given us.

She covers the whole process of writing a poem. How is a poem conceived? What are the favorable conditions of conception? Do poets work at regular hours? How do they revise? Do they accept criticisms, or not? All these questions are answered, very variously, with a number of odd and uplifting stories to illustrate them.

For instance, do you know how Walt Whitman composed? I should have expected him to write a free rhapsody, straight off, and then to revise (a little) and to excise (a little). But no. He used to write down scraps of phrases at odd moments, on odd pieces of paper, and tie them together with pieces of string, or drop them into envelopes. Then, when he felt like composing, he would keep a writing tablet on his knee, and play with his cat, and wait for the right opening. 'Suddenly he would start to write on the tablet'—and work through the scraps he had already collected, one by one, throwing them down as he finished. They were sketches, and he was now making the finished work.

There is also a valuable story about Browning. His system was 'to write down on a slate, in prose, what he wanted to say, and then turn it into verse, striving after the greatest amount of condensation possible; thus, if an exclamation suggested his meaning, he would substitute this for a whole sentence.' This may not be true of his lyrics. But surely it is true of his long dramatic pieces; and surely it reminds us of one of the chief facts about poetry, which we often forget— that it is more intense and more meaningful than prose.

Both Miss Bartlett's book and James's *Notebooks* demonstrate a valuable truth—that art is not wholly based on personal experience. Art is also based on vicarious experience. For Henry James, a story heard at a dinner table could set the imagination working. For many a poet, a book written by another man is as exciting as a love affair or a voyage of travel. There has never been a finer demonstration of this than a book published some twenty years ago and still immensely valuable, both as a piece of scholarly detective work and as a feat of beautiful, if occasionally overelaborate, imaginative writing. This is *The Road to Xanadu*, by John Livingston Lowes. A massive work, in 434 pages and 200 more of notes and index, it is so gracefully and smoothly written that it can be read (as few scholarly books can) for pleasure.

In one sentence, it is a study of the books read by Samuel

Coleridge which enabled him to write 'The Ancient Mariner' and 'Kubla Khan.' Sounds a little dull, perhaps? Perhaps it would be if 'The Ancient Mariner' and 'Kubla Khan' were not such wonderful and apparently inexplicable poems, if Coleridge had not had such a brilliant mind, if he had not read such fascinating books, and if Lowes had not had such a sympathetic style. Those of us who do not know it will have hours of delight in reading it; those who do will forgive a short visit to its enchanted pages.

We know, from Coleridge himself, what started him on the second poem. He was reading the seventeenth-century travel book *Purchas His Pilgrimage,* and fell asleep (slightly doped) over the lines

> In Xamdu did Cublai Can build a stately palace . . .

And then, in a three-hour sleep, he composed a poem two or three-hundred lines long. When he woke, he started to write it out. He was interrupted 'by a person on business from Porlock,' and all the poem, except the opening, was lost. But it begins in almost the exact words of *Purchas*:

> In Xanadu did Kubla Khan
> A stately pleasure-dome decree.

Now, since Coleridge says a book inspired him, we are justified in looking for other books which entered his dream. And Lowes has found them. Into that short poem of 54 lines Coleridge poured the following memories:

—an account of the Old Man of the Mountains, the organizer of the assassins
—several descriptions of the subtropical scenery of the southeastern United States (from Bartram's *Travels through . . . Carolina*)
—Bruce's discovery of the source of the Nile
—Milton's description of an earthly paradise in Abyssinia (also based on *Purchas*)

—a travel-tale about a moon-image of ice in Kashmir
—the Greco-Roman myth of the river Alpheus which
  flows beneath the sea (Alph)
—an ode on 'The Passions,' by Collins
—and who knows what else?

It is truly delightful to watch the skill, learning, and taste
with which Lowes traces all these diverse threads, out of the
fabric of Coleridge's poem, to so many other human minds,
and strange experiences, and romantic explorations, and moving books. Miss Bartlett tells us that the Irish poet Æ objected to such a search because it almost implied 'that when
the palette is spread with color it accounts for the masterpiece.' But in fact it implies no such thing, and Lowes is careful to say so. It does imply that, without a richly spread
palette, there could be no masterpiece. But it goes on to say
that the masterpiece also needs the painter's carefully practiced technique, and above all the lucky impetus. It stresses
the fact that at least three distinct processes are needed for a
work of art: *preparation, incubation,* and *artistic definition.*
  There are parallels for this in other activities of the mind.
Lowes quotes a strangely interesting description of scientific
thought by the distinguished mathematician Poincaré, in his
Science and Method:

(1) a period of conscious work
(2) 'inspirations' or 'new combinations' produced in
    the mind by unconscious activity
(3) calculations made from them by the conscious
    mind, acting with its usual attention and dis-
    cipline.

He points out that Darwin and Newton did not 'work out'
their theories. The theory of evolution occurred to Darwin
in a flash of vision; the apple which fell from the tree gave
Newton a conception of the laws governing the physical uni-

verse—in both cases a revelation came after long and almost prayerful preparation. And then followed the long years of careful elaboration—the same toil which Henry James expended so lavishly on his novels, and which Coleridge too often wasted on talk, or plans, or drugs, or casual callers 'on business from Porlock.'

It is in that movement that the fascination of these studies is to be found. The long preparation, infinitely various; the unseen, unfelt incubation; the rapid vision; the arduous elaboration. There lies the true understanding of art. We fail to appreciate a picture, a poem, a scientific achievement, if we regard it as a single, monolithic entity. We understand it best if we see it as the product of a process. Life is movement and change; and art, being life, is best known when we see it as movement. The poem contains the flow of thought through the dreamer's mind; the bridge is not a contractor's job, but a *being* that lives with the thought and will power which created it, and which are still somehow creating and sustaining it.

———

P. Bartlett, *Poems in Process* (Oxford, 1951).

J. L. Lowes, *The Road to Xanadu* (Houghton Mifflin, 1930).

F. O. Matthiessen and K. B. Murdock (ed.), *The Notebooks of Henry James* (Oxford, 1947).

Crime and Punishment, Sometimes

ONE horrible but fascinating part of our lives is crime. We do not all commit crime. With luck we may not even suffer it. But we are all endangered by it; at present we are all financially mulcted by it; and, judging by the newspapers and the bookstores, we are all deeply interested in it.

There are many good memorable books about crime. We are not talking of detective stories—they belong to a special class, turned out by highly trained artisans for a peculiar public. Books about crime are much broader, and approach universal literature.

Some of the greatest plays and stories in the world deal with crime: for instance, *Hamlet*; for instance, *Macbeth*; for instance, the *Oresteia* of Aeschylus; and only yesterday *Oliver Twist* and *Edwin Drood*; and *The Brothers Karamazov*; and

An American Tragedy; Faulkner's *Intruder in the Dust,* his hideous *Sanctuary,* and many more.

There are other books, less famous than these, which can still hold us in the same way. These are true stories of crime, authentic reports, usually with analyses by trained observers. The detective-story fans do not talk much about them; they are seldom reviewed by critics interested in belles-lettres; yet they are an essential part of the central stuff of literature.

Most of them deal with the one crime which for thousands of years has been thought the most terrible of all: murder. A first-rate example has lately appeared: this is *Classic Crimes,* edited by William Roughead. Mr. Roughead, who died recently, was an elderly lawyer from Edinburgh, with a pawky sense of humor, a lively intelligence, a considerable knowledge of the law, and—notwithstanding that—a strong sense of right and wrong, together with a neat, clear style, varied by odd old-fashioned words from Scotland which strike with a kindly cadence on the ear. He will not say 'administer' a drug, but 'exhibit' it; and he will tactfully describe a bad girl by saying that (in Lang's words) she was 'other than a good one.' In America the master of this particular art was the late Edmund Pearson: his masterpieces were *Studies in Murder* and *Instigation of the Devil.* His retelling of his own favorite, the Borden case from New London, Connecticut, could hardly be surpassed for pungency.

Last in this group I must name a work which is out of print and whose author is almost forgotten—because I am sure it is a good book which some enterprising publisher should resuscitate. This is William Bolitho's *Murder for Profit*—a study not of ordinary murder but of the mass murderers, such as Burke and Hare, who killed specimens for the dissecting room; G. J. Smith, who drowned his brides for their insurance and played the harmonium while they died;

Landru, the Bluebeard of the Paris suburbs; and, worst of all, Fritz Haarmann of Hanover, who was beheaded in 1925 for killing twenty-four young men, and who was more than suspected of cannibalism and other frightful sins. I visited his house in the Rothe Reihe in Hanover just seven years ago: a tall shaky tenement of lath and plaster, perhaps cemented together with blood; once the heart of a thick rookery of vice and crime, it now stands alone like a gallows. The inhabitants still remembered Haarmann. They said he was always very polite. They invited me to go upstairs and visit his room; but it was too like entering the Cabinet of Dr. Caligari.

These books are all studies of the complete case, from the time before the murder through the commission of the crime down to the end of the trial. There is an interesting variation, more complete but more limited: this is the trial report pure and simple. In Britain it is represented by a long series called *Notable British Trials,* some of which can be got here in the Penguin series, abbreviated as *Famous Trials,* edited by Harry and James Hodge. In this country a fine example has recently appeared: Quentin Reynolds' *Courtroom*—a study of the most spectacular cases defended by Samuel Leibowitz; but there is room for many more, for everyone loves a good trial.

Murder is as old as Adam's firstborn. But recently we have seen the development of a new crime—or rather an old crime whose dangers have multiplied and which has become more formidable: the crime of treason. One of the most incisive stylists now writing in English has turned her sharp eyes and her sharp pen upon the subject. This is Rebecca West. Her book, *The Meaning of Treason,* has just been reissued in England with two additional chapters on the recent atomic treason trials. I haven't seen this yet, but I hope it will include her masterly description of that brilliant scientist and political and moral idiot, Dr. Klaus Emil Fuchs. In the same class, though on a lower plane, are the recent books on the Hiss case, and the report of the Canadian spy trial which vanished with such remarkable rapidity from all possible distributing outlets. But at this point, treason books pass into books about the technique of espionage, which, as Mr. Pickwick says, 'comprises in itself a difficult study of no inconsiderable magnitude.'

There is one type of crime which, I regret to see, is scarcely represented at all in fiction or in non-fiction. This is swindling. Of course, a complicated theft has its charm, too: you may remember an excellent movie about a jewel robbery called *The Asphalt Jungle*; yet, somehow, there are not many literary descriptions of such enterprises, perhaps because too much has to be visualized. But why not write up the historic swindles? No doubt they are terribly difficult to analyze, but then that is a challenge to the writer. One of the few I know in literature is the awe-inspiring scheme by which Casanova attempted to get an aged duchess to sign over all her money to him, on the pretext that through his help as a priest of the occult powers (particularly the planets) she could pass out of existence and then be reborn as a male child, be brought up under his disinterested guardianship, and then, for a new lifetime, enjoy her own wealth and her new youth and manhood. This one failed, for some reason . . . for the usual reason . . . it failed because Casanova could never keep his mind on business when there was a girl around; but he describes it beautifully. Then Jules Romains has a good high-level swindle toward the end of his *Men of Good Will*. But still, that is fiction. Why have we no good vivid description of the Teapot Dome affair? or of . . . but this is dangerous ground.

There are many more types of crime that can, as De

Quincey said of murder, be 'considered as fine arts.' One can fill a nice little bookcase with their true stories, beginning with the *Newgate Calendar*. They make durable reading. If you have a feverish cold, without danger and without much discomfort, it is delightful to spend some hours with the fascinating and enigmatic Madeleine Smith (her lover died of repeated doses of arsenic, and the verdict was the canny Scots one of Not Proven, which has been explained as meaning 'Not Guilty, but Don't Do It Again'); or else in puzzling out that awful miscarriage of justice, the Oscar Slater case. The chief trouble is that you tend to go off your meals. After reading about the Borden murders, you seem to smell the hot mutton broth which the family had for breakfast on the last morning. After going over the Armstrong case, you begin to wonder whether the grapes at the bedside may not have been drilled open to receive a small dose of an irritant poison: the words *antimony, laudanum, strychnine* begin to ring like little bells in your ears, especially during the light meals allowed to an invalid.

Now, seriously, where lies the interest in crime books? Don't you think it has several different sources?

First, there is the crime in which the chief agent is unknown. This is a question without a visible answer. In Shakespeare's *Henry VI,* the body of the Duke of Gloucester is brought in, and the fatal question is put with stately eloquence:

> But see, his face is black and full of blood,
> His eyeballs further out than when he lived,
> Staring full ghastly like a strangled man:
> His hair upreared, his nostrils stretched with struggling;
> His hands abroad displayed, as one that grasped
> And tugged for life, and was by strength subdued.

CRIME / 199

Look on the sheets: his hair, you see, is sticking,
His well-proportioned beard made rough and rugged,
Like to the summer's corn by tempest lodged.*
It cannot be but he was murdered here.
The least of all these signs were probable.

The act is clear; but the actor and the motive are unknown. The classical case of this is surely *The Brothers Karamazov,* in which the real murderer is discovered only toward the end, the man who is found guilty feels guilty, but is not wholly guilty, and other people (unconnected with the action) feel guilty, too. In fact, many a reader has also wished to murder old man Karamazov. And there is a week's good reading in Browning's poetic analysis of a murder case, *The Ring and the Book*: where a seventeenth-century murder is examined again and again with the most subtle care from every point of view: we end by feeling that the whole truth can never be known to men, and only to God.

Next, the motive is sometimes a puzzle. It is impossible to understand *why* this man, or this woman, would conceive and execute an atrocious and complex crime. Hence the interest of murder. We can all imagine why a man would rob Brink's, but not so easily why a man would kill a comparative stranger. (This is part of the attraction of going to trials. We sit in court, and look at the accused, who seem to be so ordinary, mere subway characters, passionless, devoted to routine, not very brainy; and yet they seem to have planned the satisfaction of outrageous appetites in a powerful, novel, and intricate manner.) In fiction, the finest of these books is *Crime and Punishment*. There is a fairly good treatment of a quiet little mass-murderer by Jules Romains, in the story of Quinette which runs through the first part of his *Men of*

---

* i.e. laid flat or torn up.

Good Will, and which displays the career of a man who begins to like murder as others begin to love gambling, or writing poetry.

Then again, the puzzle may arise after the crime has been committed, and discovered, and understood. (This is one of the errors of the usual detective story, which is apt to assume that as soon as the mysterious murderer has been arrested, he will be convicted: although Nero Wolfe sometimes, wisely, anticipates the processes of justice.) There are many complex cases in which the evidence points with a steady finger at one person, and yet it is impossible for the jury to find that person guilty. So it was with Raskolnikov in *Crime and Punishment,* and that is why the police inspector had to spend so many days extracting a confession from him by psychological pressure. Sometimes, again, the jury is idiotic. 'Poor boy!' they will say of a hardened tough of twenty, and very often, 'Poor girl,' of a sinister harpy of twenty-five. Sometimes also they have been bamboozled by a clever defense lawyer, and sometimes let down by a careless or crooked prosecutor.

But above all these motives for interest, or beneath them, there is something deeper, an indefinable sense of wonder. When I was invited to see Haarmann's rooms, I said that it was like visiting the Cabinet of Dr. Caligari . . . penetrating into something like systematized madness, crazed logic. So it is with all big murders. That is why they differ from killing in war, or its older brother, killing in hot-blooded dueling. Murder and the more elaborate crimes are not usually committed by maniacs. Yet they take us into those recesses of the mind where the reason is not the ruler, but the servant. And that is the region where poetry and the arts also come to birth. (Thomas Mann believes that the artist is opposed to his own society in the same way as a sick man or a criminal; and Oscar Wilde, himself in opposition, wrote an essay on the artist who also was a poisoner.) It is a strange experience to visit that region, like going down in a diving helmet into a world which is one's own and yet seems to be largely unexplored and unpossessed. When you come up, you will still feel the distinction between right and wrong. But you may well be prepared to say (in the first few minutes at least) that some novels and poems are felonies; that certain paintings and buildings ought to be tried for atrocious assault; and that several faces which you know are the faces of criminals, waiting for a crime to commit.

———

W. Bolitho, *Murder for Profit* (Harper, 1926).

F. M. Dostoevsky, *The Brothers Karamazov* (tr. C. Garnett, Grosset & Dunlap, n.d.).

F. M. Dostoevsky, *Crime and Punishment* (tr. C. Garnett, Macmillan, 1937).

H. and J. Hodge, *Notable British Trials* (Penguin).

E. Pearson, *The Borden Case* (Doubleday, 1937).

E. Pearson, *Instigation of the Devil* (Scribner, 1930).

E. Pearson, *Studies in Murder* (Macmillan, 1924).

Q. Reynolds, *Courtroom* (Farrar, Straus, 1950).

J. Romains, *Men of Good Will* (tr. W. B. Wells and G. Hopkins, Knopf, 1934-46).

W. Roughead, *Classic Crimes* (British Book Center, 1952).

R. West, *The Meaning of Treason* (Viking, 1947).

Narcissus the Novelist

W
HAT is a novel?

It used to be easy enough to say what a novel was. It was a long story, an invented tale about non-existent people. It was both true, and not-true. The people never existed, and their actions never happened; and yet the people were recognizably real as types, and what they did was supposed to fit into the pattern of real events which made their particular milieu and period. Take one of the finest novels ever written, Dostoevsky's *Crime and Punishment*. There never was a young student called Raskolnikov who murdered an old money lender from motives he thought were idealistic, and then was persuaded by a magistrate into confessing. But that kind of thing did happen in Russia. Or could happen. Generally, the story was true. In particular detail, it was not-true.

So a novel used to be fiction pretending it was truth. The trick of writing a novel—or one of the tricks—used to be keeping up the pretense. Sometimes one of the characters would pretend to be telling the entire story as a narrative of actual happenings. You know the kind of historical romance that begins:

> My dear children, I set down these facts now that my life is drawing to its close, for I am one of the few survivors of that small but gallant band which invaded Canada in 1812 . . .

That was the pattern. But recently, more and more in the past few years, we have been getting a new type of novel. Instead of being fiction dressed up as truth, this is the opposite. It is truth dressed up as fiction. Only the names and sometimes the places are changed. Ninety-five times out of a hundred, this novel is an autobiography. So many such novels have come out recently that it is possible to see the patterns into which they fall.

1. The commonest is the Thomas Wolfe type: *My Family and How I Grew Up*. The hero of this is very sensitive, surrounded by boors who misunderstand his aspirations, try to brutalize him, and partly succeed, until he tears himself loose, and, like some proud ship sailing, breaks out of the marshy inlets and foul stagnant harbors of home into the vast free ocean. (There are two good titles, *Vast Free Ocean* and *Proud Ship Sailing*.) Often an important part of this story is a passionate but disappointing initiation into *s e x*. And so is a series of enlarged and hand-colored portraits of Aunt Flora, Uncle Fauna, and other relatives. Apparently John Steinbeck's new book, *East of Eden,* started out like this; and then, half way through, the colors got brighter and cruder till the whole thing turned into melodrama.

2. The next commonest type of autobiographical novel at present is the story about the sensitive soldier: *How I Suffered in the Armed Forces*. This is not the broad panorama of warfare that one gets in a big job like *War and Peace,* or Zweig's *The Case of Sergeant Grischa* (one of the best books about the First World War). No, this is the f64, pinpoint-focus book, not so much a story as a set of reminiscences. I think it began about thirty years ago with Sassoon's *Memoirs of a Fox-Hunting Man* and Remarque's *All Quiet*; and now it has multiplied itself. You recall James Jones's *From Here to Eternity,* Norman Mailer's well-written but basically false *Naked and the Dead*, Monsarrat's *The Cruel Sea*, and lots of stories about the Air Force.

3. Third comes a type which I personally find more interesting and more moving: autobiographical novels by members of minority groups. For instance, by a Negro (Ralph Ellison's *Invisible Man*); or by a first- or early-second-generation immigrant (I suppose the James T. Farrell books about Chicago Irish are the best known); or by a Jew (Koestler's *Thieves in the Night*). Often it is only through books like these that one can really tell *how* members of a minority live, and think, and suffer. There is an indescribable pathos about them if the little group (Saroyan's Assyrians) is disappearing even while we read about it.

4. Fourth are the reminiscences of psychological misfits. *The Snake Pit* and Hervé Bazin's *Head against the Wall* are novels which tell what it is like to be mad. Proust's novel is largely about his own world of inverts, both disguised and revealed. More and more authors lately seem to be treating the public as though it were a psychiatrist.

5. There is also the travel tale, in which the narrator, handsome, witty, irresistible, and usually rich, invades a strange country, describes its scenery and customs, makes love

to its most beautiful women, and emerges in triumph bearing 1000 pages of notes and some crumpled love tokens. Byron began this, with *Childe Harold* and *Don Juan*. In prose, Pierre Loti built a reputation on it; so did Paul Morand; there is a funny book about such a visit to these United States, called *Juan in America,* by Eric Linklater. Nowadays, such books tend not to be triumphant, but to be embittered and rather hung-over, like Hemingway's *The Sun Also Rises.* We can expect a larger flood of them from the explorers and expatriates of this, the second postwar period.

Of course, I am not deploring the passion for writing autobiographies and calling them novels. Nor am I saying it is entirely new. There is a lot of personal reminiscence in many regular novels, *David Copperfield* and *The Charterhouse of Parma.* But what *is* new nowadays is that many writers are abandoning the attempt to describe a complete segment of the world, a harmonious pattern of social life or adventure. Instead, they simply describe themselves, surround the central figure with faintly sketched or fantastically exaggerated subordinate characters, and, in the delight of reminiscence, forget the duty of telling a story.

And then, reading these books seems to be rather different from reading regular novels. Different emotions are called into play. Different critical standards are set up.

To begin with, instead of the pleasure we normally have in following the development of a fictional character, say Kim or Julien Sorel, we have the meaner thrill of eavesdropping, of hearing secrets, of identifying real people and reading revelations about them—something close to the base delights of reading another man's mail or listening on a party line. In Proust, the experts can identify all the chief characters, beginning with that eminent monster, Robert de Montesquiou. Often the author makes this easier by choosing easily penetrable names. Thus, if John Smith's psychiatrist cures him of kleptomania, he is apt to write a novel about a kleptomaniac and call the hero *Joe Sm*art, or *James Black* (Black-Smith, see?). Sometimes—and this is the most embarrassing of all—sometimes the author supplies facts about himself, to be printed in the blurb on the jacket, which coincide so neatly with the details in the novel that we know he wants us to identify him with the leading personage. He wants to tell us that it was he, really he, who had all these disgraceful, but exciting, adventures.

And yet, in spite of all this self-revelation, such novels are rarely complete. They hide things, they suppress evidence. The hero or heroine rarely reasons and doubts and decides as we do before doing something important. He or she acts . . . and then emotes afterward. The long brooding and the careful planning which go on in such minds are seldom described. Proust was in fact a very shrewd operator, who knew what he wanted in several different fields and went out for it; but the hero of his book looks like a sleepwalker, and his grand adventure is so disguised as to be unintelligible. Also, in nearly all such books, other people are not shown as three-dimensional figures, with lives of their own. They are shown as friends or enemies of the hero, objects of his love or hate or fear. I don't know if you have ever visited a prison or an asylum. If you have, you will remember how some of the inmates glance at you with a pretty normal expression, sizing you up as people do in a railroad station. Others don't look at you at all, absorbed in their own misery. But there are always some who gaze at you with the fixity and intensity of a cat watching a bird. Quite clearly, they are thinking, 'How can I *use* this person? Will he help me to escape? Can

I convince him, or dominate him?' Through eyes like these, the autobiographical novelist often sees his friends and relatives, and his novel is often like a single large heroic statue surrounded by caricatures.

Another difficulty about these books is their shapelessness. Since the author remembers everything, and thinks that everything about himself is important, he often tries to put everything down. Joyce's *Ulysses* attempts to record all the sights, sounds, and events of Dublin on 16 June 1904, although most of them are hideously boring. They say that the chief problem in Thomas Wolfe's work was that he could not stop. He would write several hundred thousand words of total recall. He would take this to his editor, Maxwell Perkins. Perkins would cut out several large sections and put them in the deep freeze; he would reduce the rest to chapters, and mold them into a novel. Sometimes he would ask Wolfe to write a bridge-passage of some eight or ten thousand words to fill in a gap. Wolfe would go away and come back with another 200,000 words, all hot and steaming from the volcanoes of the subconscious. A regular novel, when good, is clearly and subtly constructed. An autobiographical novel is often formless, lacking both inward balance and outward harmony.

Still, such books have one great advantage. They may be shapeless. Most of them have no proper ending, and few of them balance their developments and their crises. They may be distorted: their authors usually have a grudge or an obsession. But they *sound real*. They are based on real life. So many conventional novels, for all their balance and neatness, sound painfully artificial, laboriously contrived by a dutiful workman turning out his thirtieth or fortieth trademarked product. They are read only as fiction, only as something to pass the time and kill the pain: aspirin in chewing gum.

Wodehouse is still at it: the comic peer who breeds pigs, the comic butler, the formidable old virago . . . heavens, how tedious it is! Poor Angela Thirkell, gossiping away year after year about the elegant gentleman and the sensitive ladies of Barsetshire, 400 pages with not a single new emotion, and always ending with a suitable marriage between two properly connected young people. And then the novelists of the immediate past! Walpole! Galsworthy! Bennett! Robert W. Chambers! Almost impossible to read now, even as entertainment. One of my ideas of purgatory would be to be snowed in for the winter in northwestern Montana, with nothing in the cabin to read except the works of—Brrr. No, the autobiographers usually have only one book to write—although they may publish it in several sections. But it springs from life, and not from bored repetition of a basically artificial trick. And therefore the autobiographical novel is half of a good book. The danger is that its author may forget to do the other half of the work. For the great novelists are those who combine memory with perception and imagination, who are interested not only in themselves but in all the world, who not only relive their own lives but create new people who will live long after they themselves have ceased to enjoy this short, this transient life.

H. Bazin, *Head against the Wall* (tr. W. J. Strachan, Prentice Hall, 1952).

R. Ellison, *Invisible Man* (Random House, 1952).

E. Hemingway, *The Sun Also Rises* (Scribner, 1926).

J. Jones, *From Here to Eternity* (Scribner, 1951).

A. Koestler, *Thieves in the Night* (Macmillan, 1946).

E. Linklater, *Juan in America* (Cape, London, 1931).

N. Mailer, *The Naked and the Dead* (Rinehart, 1948).

N. Monsarrat, *The Cruel Sea* (Knopf, 1951).

E. M. Remarque, *All Quiet on the Western Front* (tr. A. Wheen, Little Brown, 1929).

S. Sassoon, *Memoirs of a Fox-Hunting Man* (Coward McCann, 1929).

J. Steinbeck, *East of Eden* (Viking, 1952).

M. J. Ward, *The Snake Pit* (Random House, 1946).

A. Zweig, *The Case of Sergeant Grischa* (tr. E. Sutton, Viking, 1928).

The Museum without Walls

_____

Do you remember the first book you ever handled? What sort of book was it?

I think I can remember mine. It was a picture book. That must have been more than forty years ago; but I can see it now. It was a big fat bound volume called (I think) *The Picture Magazine*. It was really an ancestor of today's *Life* magazine, full of pictures from all over the world—mostly engravings, hardly any photographs, if I remember correctly (it was an old volume), but clear businesslike drawings well reproduced, with some explanatory text which I could not read. It had nothing so beautiful as *Life's* splendid reproductions of pictures and colored photographs of scenery; but it ranged very widely: drawings of Chinese cities, battles in the Sudan and East Asia, curious inventions, disasters like the sinking of the ferryboat *General Slocum,* and engravings of interesting paintings new and old.

Most of us have probably had a similar experience. Most of us probably remember a picture book as one of our earliest and best books. And that kind of book is not for children only. Some of the finest books in the world are picture books. I can think of two right away: the famous manuscript of the Gospels illuminated and decorated by Irish artists, called the *Book of Kells* (there is a current reproduction of it by a Swiss firm which costs several hundred dollars, and which I should dearly love to own), and the wonderful prayer book made by two artists who worked over it for about ten years, *Les Très-Riches Heures du Duc de Berry.*

However, there is one type of picture book which is meant to be permanent, and which I believe is particularly important. André Malraux has written eloquently about it, and produced a good example of what it might become. He calls it the Museum without Walls. This is the art book—wholly or largely composed of photographs of distinguished paintings, sculpture, etchings, illuminations, architecture, pottery, and other expressions of man's enjoyment of the pleasures of sight. It is usually rather expensive; it is extremely hard to produce, for the process of color reproduction is painfully complicated and costly; but when well done it is a joy to possess. People who tend to read almost too much can find a new sort of pleasure in simply sitting for an hour, looking at pictures of beautiful things. Recently I was turning over an album of photographs of Notre Dame Cathedral, and found myself gazing at a thirteenth-century statue of the Virgin Mary, serene, exquisite, queenly, with the pillar breaking out into leaves above her head and her robe falling in harmonious curves to her feet. I looked at it for many minutes, not really thinking, but rather *feeling,* as one does when listening to a good string quartet.

And of course there is another tremendous advantage in such books, the advantage stressed by Malraux in his title. It is that most of us are out of touch with great works of art: we live too far away from museums, and even when we do go to a gallery we get easily tired, and harassed by its crowds, and oppressed by its solemnity; but with a book of reproductions we can sit at home, and listen to music, and look at a painting for as long as we like—for an hour without fatigue, or for five seconds without guilt.

I own quite a number of these art books, and I have been turning them over recently. We really are lucky nowadays to be able to get fine reproductions. This time last century all we could have commanded would have been engravings in black and white, or perhaps lithographs. You remember Browning's poem, 'A Likeness':

> I keep my prints, an imbroglio,
> Fifty in one portfolio.
> When somebody tries my claret . . .
> Then I exhibit my treasure.
> After we've turned over twenty
> And—

(here is a typical Browning rhyme, daring and comic)

> —the debt of wonder my crony owes
> Is paid to my Marc Antonios,
> He stops me . . .

Browning's friend had only prints, you see; but we have books of photographs (not to mention large reproductions for our walls) which do bear a pretty close resemblance to the originals; and they seem to be improving all the time.

Such books have two chief purposes. The first of these is well enough shown in Malraux' three volumes. (They are called *Museum without Walls, The Creative Act,* and *The Twilight of the Absolute,* number 24 in the Bollingen Series,

translated by Stuart Gilbert and published by Pantheon.)
This purpose is to display before us and to explain as far as
possible what Malraux calls the common artistic heritage of
mankind. As you turn over these three massive volumes you
are confronted now with a fetish from the New Hebrides
Islands, looking like a fiend; now with a portrait from a
Greco-Egyptian coffin, looking almost exactly like an Egyp-
tian lady of today; now with a succession of statues of the
Buddha, in which we can watch the eyes gradually closing as
his meditations become deeper and his approach to enlighten-
ment grows closer; now with a late Gothic head of Christ at
prayer, almost unbearably haggard, strained, distorted, and
tragic; now with Van Meegeren's forgeries of Vermeer paints;
and now with a staggeringly beautiful religious picture by the
almost unknown baroque artist, Georges de Latour. It becomes clear that Malraux' aim is to display and to explain
the art of the whole world on almost every level, from the
prehistoric cave-painting to the contemporary caricature; to
draw parallels between the art of different places and times,
which will serve both to deepen our understanding of the
works of art themselves and to interpret something of the
creative process within the artist's mind; and to explore
the peculiar relation of artists to their society and to one
another.

Does he achieve this enormous task?

Not fully. Grateful as we are for the reproductions of many
fine things we should never otherwise have seen, we must
admit that he has not chosen a representative cross-section of
the art of the world. There is a terrifying gold mask from
Mexico, and one or two other pre-Columbian objects; but not
nearly enough Aztec, Mayan, and Peruvian work. Baroque
art is the art of the almost-too-much; and there is almost too
much of it here. There is a lot of fine Indian and Siamese,

but not enough Chinese, Japanese, and Tibetan; and not nearly enough Greek vase-painting and Roman portraiture.

Then I found the book very hard to read and understand. It is not a continuous argument so much as a series of affirmations, often very cryptic. It is scarcely possible to carry on a dialogue with the author—as one usually can when reading such a book. One must simply remain silent, and listen to Malraux uttering loud abstractions.

Mr. Gilbert's translation does not do much to help. Consider this sentence:

> It is on the cards that, thanks to a process of metamorphosis, Picasso may come to be regarded, in the year 2200, as a compeer of the Persian ceramists.

Something of the difficulty here is apparently the fault of the translator: you cannot have a slang phrase like 'on the cards,' an archaism like 'compeer,' and a technicality like 'ceramists' in the same sentence. But the cryptic quality of the book springs chiefly from a conflict in the author, in Malraux himself. He has acknowledged this by revising the whole thing. I understand that the new version, called *Les Voies du silence,* has about 300 changes and is far better proportioned. He has, it appears, been trying not to discuss world art with you and me, but rather to argue about it with the shades of the German historians Frobenius and Spengler. Difficult for him; almost unintelligible for us.

But this is not to say that the book is worthless. It is full of lovely things and stimulating ideas: it is interesting to keep and to wander through; even though it still needs arrangement, it is a rich Museum without Walls.

Three of my colleagues at Columbia have made a more compact and complete museum: *A History of World Art,* by

Upjohn, Wingert, and Mahler. It is surprisingly well written for a manual produced by a group. The authors know that it is not enough to give students information about works of art (or literature, or music); you must also show them that much knowledge means pleasure, means fulfillment of a need. It, too, has its gaps: not nearly enough on folk art and savage art, the whole thing heavily Western and European in slant. But I learned a vast amount from reading it.

The pictures are small, and are only in monochrome, which wrecks many of them. The singing angels from the Van Eyck altar occupy a page; but from that black and white copy you would hardly guess that their robes gleam and glitter with warm hues, and almost seem to sing like their voices. That so much of the beauty and interest of most of the originals survives is a tribute to their power; but so much has been lost that it saddens me, as a bad translation saddens me.

These are extensive books. Their aim is to cover a wide area. But picture books may also give us intension, telling us more about one particular school, explaining one particular artist. This is a very important point. If we see (with the usual onlooker's eye) one or two paintings by Goya or Leonardo, we have seen external objects . . . interesting, but detached, incomplete. If we look at a book of all their works, we can begin to read their minds.

Such an album is Ludwig von Baldass' book on Bosch (published in Vienna); such is Gustav Glück's fine collection of the paintings of Breughel. The finest work of this kind published in America is surely Erwin Panofsky's magnificent two-volume study of Albrecht Dürer. The work came out in 1943; it went into a second edition in 1945, and it is now in its third. Princeton University Press, the publishers, have done a beautiful job of typography and reproduction.

Much of the second volume is a tremendous list of all Dürer's work, with cross-indexes, concordance, and so on: the proof, and the basis, of sound scholarship. The rest of it is a collection of 300 fine reproductions of Dürer's most characteristic pieces, together with some of the models which were in his head when he composed them. The entire first volume is a biography of the artist, together with a close analysis of his technical and spiritual life. Dr. Panofsky is one of the few scholars who can really enter into the mind of a perplexed, partly mad, versatile genius, working through mystical emblems, lofty but illogical religious beliefs, and obscure, now obsolete, theories of the relation between man and the ideal and God; who can display how all this rich intellectual activity was translated, by laboriously acquired and devoutly practiced craft, into permanent works of art; and who can extend this into a contemplation of the turmoil of an entire age like the Renaissance, and of the entire process of artistic creation.

Elsewhere we have discussed another such scholar: the late John Livingstone Lowes, with his miraculous exploration, *The Road to Xanadu.* Panofsky's book is a greater work, on a greater subject. And yet, as I read his chapter on the strange engraving called *The First Melancholy* I was reminded again and again of the Ancient Mariner, and the nightmare Death-in-Life, and the caves of ice, and the antarctic seas which Lowes penetrated in pursuit of that haunted ship, the mind of Coleridge.

A book like Panofsky's *Dürer* has many inestimable virtues. One of the highest is simply this. It takes you inside the mind of a great artist. It shows you that he is a greater man than you. It shows you why. It shows you, it makes visible in the boldest way, the manifold inhabitants of the world of his sight and his imagination. One play by Shakespeare may be trifling, like *Love's Labour's Lost,* or repellent, like *Timon of*

Athens. But his complete works are a universe which would contain many thousands of minds like ours. Not only are such mind-universes thickly populated; they are full of terrible wars. When we look at Dürer's pictures, and read Dr. Panofsky's explanation of the events and the symbolism which met to produce them, we realize that art is not (as some of us think) merely decoration. It is, for many artists, an immense but difficult spiritual victory: a series of victories in an endless war. However eccentric, gloomy, or repulsive it may sometimes appear, art is a harmony which man imposes upon this often brutal and irrational world, in order that he may understand it; even when it is almost unbearable, endure it; and ultimately, although it howls around him like the Furies in tragedy, ultimately love it.

L. von Baldass, *Hieronymus Bosch* (Schroll, Vienna, 1943).

G. Glück, *Bruegels Gemälde* (Schroll, Vienna, 4th ed., 1937).

A. Malraux, *The Psychology of Art* (3 volumes, tr. S. Gilbert, Bollingen Series XXIV, Pantheon Books, New York, n.d.).

E. Panofsky, *Albrecht Dürer* (Princeton University Press, 3rd ed., 1948).

E. M. Upjohn, P. S. Wingert, and J. G. Mahler, *History of World Art* (Oxford University Press, New York, 1949).

The Art of Translation

SURELY translation is an art, and a difficult one. How complex and subtle a writer's mind must be, to penetrate the entire meaning of another writer, working in a foreign language, and then to transfer that meaning into his own tongue! The process is hard enough when the two writers are contemporaries, working in neighboring languages, like English and French. But it becomes far harder when the languages are remote from each other in structure and background, like English and Chinese, or modern French and classical Greek. Thought and speech are not two different things which are casually connected, like a motor car and its driver. They are intricately interlinked like cause and effect, like form and substance, so that a thought expressed in two different ways is practically two different thoughts. The translator therefore, when he is working from a remote language, has somehow to *re-think* the thoughts of the original, in order to express them in his own tongue. If I may mention my own experience, I should say that doing such a job of translation is actually more difficult than writing an original work. And a third difficulty, a third barrier may exist: the barrier of time. You and I, if we set out to translate a modern author like Franz Kafka or Jules Romains, would find his mind hard to penetrate and his style hard to reproduce; but we should feel that we at least inhabited the same spiritual climate, used similar rules of logic, felt kindred emotions. But if we attempted to translate someone distant from us in time, like Dante, like St. Paul, like Lady Murasaki, we should discover again and again that the mind of such an author was shaped by a society and an age so vastly different from our own that it would become almost impossible to re-think his thoughts. Almost . . . but never utterly impossible: for the greatest pleasure of literature is to feel the truth that, in spite of huge distances in time and apparently impenetrable barriers of language, the thoughts and emotions of all mankind can still be permanently expressed by great writers and understood by diligent and sympathetic readers.

Translation, then, is an art; and a difficult art. But it has long been, and often still is, a sadly neglected one. It has been underpaid, and despised, and misunderstood, and frequently botched and hurried. The worst result of that neglect is that it keeps us from knowing and appreciating really good things, just as a poor black and white photograph of a great painting, or an inexpert student's copy of it, may deform and spoil our understanding of the painter's greatness. Let us take one or two examples.

Suppose we go to the opera. We choose *La Traviata*—the title means nothing to anyone unless he understands Italian, and ought to be translated. We buy a libretto, printed in the original Italian with an English translation. We look through it, and arrive at Act Four, where poor Violetta is dying. She rises and tries to dress. To her maid she says, 'Annina, dammi a vestire.' This is translated as 'Annina, my dress bring hither.' On the same page we find a jolly band of revelers passing beneath her window: they are leading a prize ox to be killed and roasted. The song comes through the window. In Italian it sounds jolly. In translation it begins

> Room for the quadruped
> Fattest and fairest!

Of course, if you read and understand Italian, these phrases are merely silly. But if you don't, they are discouraging, even disgusting. You might very well conclude, as some have done, that *La Traviata* was a silly piece, and that opera was a silly occupation for a serious person. You would of course be wrong, but your mistake would have been caused by reading a bad translation.

Or think of the Bible. The first sentences of the Gospel according to St. John, as translated into English, are these:

> In the beginning was the Word, and the Word was with God, and the Word was God. The same was in the beginning with God.

We read this, and ask ourselves what it means. Does it mean that the Word of God—the Bible itself—has always existed? No, it cannot possibly mean that. Does it mean that speech always existed in the mind of God before human language was created? or that some specific utterance sums up the whole of God's nature? That, too, is very hard to believe. One could think about these puzzling sentences for many months without penetrating to their true meaning, because they have been mistranslated—not only by the English translators but by St. Jerome, who turned them into Latin for the early Church. It is almost impossible to translate them, because the idea intended and its name do not co-exist in Latin or in English. But if I were to make an effort to give their true meaning I think I should say, 'In the beginning was Reason,' or 'In the beginning there was *articulate thought.*' Robert Bridges boldly put forward this translation: 'In the beginning was Mind.'

Now, these two cases are only small examples. But see how they interfere with our knowledge and our appreciation. What are we to say of big mistranslations? What can we think when we see that a mighty and permanent work like a Greek tragedy is lost to us because it has not been adequately translated? How much do we lose? We are surrounded by great and beautiful books and poems in French and Spanish and Hebrew and Greek and Japanese and Arabic and many other languages; and we are deaf and blind to them, because they have never been made to speak in a tongue we can understand and in terms we can enjoy. Recently the most famous Italian novel was newly translated into English: *The Betrothed* by Alessandro Manzoni, rendered by Alexander Colquhoun. The reviewers nearly all welcomed it, and nearly all said that—although the book is over a century old—it came to them as brand-new and newly delightful because it had now been well translated for the first time. How many other masterpieces have been withheld from us?

There is one field where this difficulty is particularly striking, and where valiant efforts are now being made to amend it. This is the field of translation from the Greek and Latin classics. Not many of us know Greek and Latin nowadays: but the demand for good translations of the greatest works of Greece and Rome is constantly increasing. Random House has sold about 100,000 copies of its translations of the *Iliad* and the *Odyssey*, and I understand that E. V. Rieu's version of the *Odyssey* (Penguin) has sold no less than 300,000 in this country. All over the United States, courses in the Humanities, or the Essential Books, or the Literatures of the World, or the Classics in Translation, are being introduced in colleges, and nearly always welcomed. At Columbia the Humanities course, instituted by John Erskine, has exposed nearly twenty generations of students to the minds of Homer and Lucretius and Dante and Montaigne—all in translation: and they have thriven on it. You will know also of the many discussion groups which have grown up outside colleges, and how eagerly they seek out decent renderings of the great books, to read and to analyze. The demand for good translations is actually far greater than the supply.

We have discussed the various difficulties of translation. There is still another, which is permanent. It is that the great books usually have to be translated, not once, but again and again, into modern languages—because the modern languages change and their styles and poetic idioms change. To take an easy example, it is rather repulsive nowadays to read Greek tragedies as translated into the blank verse and the poetic vocabulary of the mid-nineteenth century. Our use of meter, our sentence rhythms, our feeling for words and phrases have all changed in the last thirty years or so; and it is not enough today for the translator of Euripides to know Greek—he must also be steeped in the dramatic verse of T. S. Eliot and Chrisopher Fry and others. If no contemporary idiom exists for the work to be translated, then the translator's task is harder, for he will have to create one.

Difficult, difficult. Yes, but it has been done, and it is being done today. For one of the qualities of great books is this:

they have the power, when you live with them, to make you greater, to deepen your thought, and expand your powers of speech. They take possession of you, and, if you are tasteful and industrious and lucky, they speak through you.

Before we go on to look at some of the most interesting translations of the past few years, let me point out one peculiarity of great books which we must all have noticed. This is that they are so rich, so various, so deep and complex that they mean many different things to different people. Therefore there can be—there *must* be—many different translations of them. No two actors can ever play Hamlet in the same way: think of the vast difference between the characterizations of Barrymore, of Gielgud, of Evans, of Olivier. Similarly, no two men can ever translate Homer or Dante in the same way. It follows that, if we cannot read the original, we ought to use not one translation but several. A few years ago I was reading Dante with my son. He read the prose translation in the Modern Library, and I read Longfellow's verse translation (sometimes also attempting my own rendering direct from the Italian), and in that way we came much closer to the meaning than we could have done by looking through one window alone. If Dorothy Sayers' new translation had been available then, we should have used that too.

The biggest challenge to any translator is of course one of the best poems in the world: the *Iliad* of Homer. It is a huge work, many thousands of lines long. It is written in a splendid meter, far stronger and more varied than English blank verse. Its language is both clear and complicated, like a Beethoven symphony or a great cathedral; and it is trenchantly expressive, full of brief phrases which, once heard, can never be forgotten, but which therefore are the despair of the translator. Its range is wide, moving all the way from a crying baby to a god roaring with fury, from a wily diplomatic speech to a savage hand-to-hand battle. It is full of action and passion, myth and history, psychology and rhetoric; it is full of music. It is a world.

Undaunted by that challenge, four or five translators in the past few years have set out to turn Homer into English. And they have all been successful, working on different levels and for different purposes.

The most ambitious is the verse rendering by Richmond Lattimore, published by the University of Chicago Press. Mr. Lattimore (who is professor of Greek at Bryn Mawr) has prepared himself for his task by years of study and practice. He began about ten years ago with a version of the fearfully difficult lyric poems of Pindar. Then he translated the most difficult of all Greek plays, the *Agamemnon* of Aeschylus. This was good training, and it rewarded him. He is not merely a translator, but an original poet, with a spare, muscular, energetic style of his own. In order to make a poem worthy of Homer, he had to render this style more subtle and more freely moving, and at the same time to find a regular rhythm to reproduce the majestic regularity of Homer's epic verse. He did this by choosing a spacious meter. Not the usual English verse, which with its five beats is not roomy enough to contain all that Homer got into his lines, but the same six-beat meter which Robert Bridges used in 1929 for *The Testament of Beauty*; and then he made it lighter and swifter. Bridges was writing a didactic poem in the slow, thoughtful style of Lucretius; Lattimore was writing a strongly moving epic. Here, for comparison, are two passages from their work.

First, Bridges, from *The Testament of Beauty* (3.354-8):

> How was November's melancholy endear'd to me
> in the effigy of plowteams following and recrossing
> patiently the desolat landscape from dawn to dusk,

as the slow-creeping ripple of their single furrow
submerged the sodden litter of summer's festival!

And now, Lattimore (4.422f.):

As when along the thundering beach the surf of the sea
strikes
beat upon beat as the west wind drives it onward; far
out
cresting first on the open water, it drives thereafter
to smash roaring along the dry land, and against the
rock jut
bending breaks itself into crests spewing back the salt
wash;
so thronged beat upon beat the Danaans' close bat-
talions
steadily into battle.

You see how rapid and strong it is, and how clearly it repro-
duces the divine clarity of Homer. If Mr. Lattimore's translation has a weakness, it is perhaps that it lacks something of
the gusto and plenitude of Homer. The *Iliad* is full of sun-
shine and sweat, knotted muscles and brown skins: its words
have color and savor. Mr. Lattimore's translation wants
something of that richness, partly because the general poetic
vocabulary available in English today is much smaller than
that of Homer—or, for that matter, of Shakespeare. But it is
a clear, courageous, and successful piece of work, for which
he deserves much gratitude.

Last year a verse translation of another great poem was
isued. This is the version of Vergil's *Aeneid* by Rolfe
Humphries, published by Scribner. Like Mr. Lattimore's
Iliad, this is simpler than its original, and its author freely
admits he has cut a little. But the most interesting change is
that he has speeded up the poem. Vergil is not like Homer.

The *Aeneid* is a slow, elaborate poem, full of half lights, and obscure double and triple meanings, and haunting sound effects, and peculiar distortions of language (to which one of his most eminent contemporaries bitterly objected as 'affectation'). It does not march on with the tread of an army or gallop like a chariot, as Homer does: it is the record of a pilgrimage, arduous and thoughtful, full of anxious pauses. Now, such effects are almost impossible to reproduce in a modern language, and perhaps they ought not to be attempted. Mr. Humphries has chosen not to echo them; his style is much more brisk and carefree than Vergil's; he likes short, stabbing sentences, and bold unequivocal utterance. Here is a soldier's speech, rendered roughly as Vergil says it (2.387-91):

> Comrades, where fortune first points a way to safety and where she shows herself friendly, let us follow: let us change our shields and fit on ourselves the emblems of the Greeks. Treachery or courage, who would ask which, in an enemy? They themselves will give us weapons.

And here is Mr. Humphries' version:

> Comrades, where fortune
> First shows the way and sides with us, we follow.
> Let us change our shields, put on the Grecian emblems!
> All's fair in war: we lick them or we trick them,
> And what's the odds?

As you see, this has one mistake in it ('we follow' for 'let us follow'), one piece of slang ('lick them'), one addition ('what's the odds?'), and one omission ('They themselves will give us weapons'). But the meaning is nearly the same, and the speed and pace of the original have been increased: we can almost hear the desperate youngster shouting. Again and again, comparing Mr. Humphries' version with the original, we see him abbreviating and simplifying, but always so as to make the poem more rapid and more continuously readable. The result is that much of the poetry and music has been sacrificed, but the rhythm, the story, and the imagination are kept alive. Mark Van Doren says it is the most readable English version since Dryden, and I agree with him.

Another translation of the *Aeneid* has been completed more recently, by Mr. Cecil Day Lewis, now Professor of Poetry at Oxford University. Here is his version of the same few lines we have already looked at:

> Comrades, let's follow up where fortune has first shown us
> A way to survival, and play our luck while it is good!
> Change shields with these dead Greeks, put on their badges and flashes!
> Craft or courage—who cares, when an enemy has to be beaten?
> The Greeks themselves shall equip us.

This reads fairly well at first. But, as we reread, and continue through the rest of Mr. Lewis' rendering, we find that he has not solved the chief problem nearly so well as Mr. Humphries and others: he has not managed to blend the colloquial and the poetic. For instance, even in this little piece, 'badges and flashes' is pure British military slang, while 'craft and courage' is graceful rhetoric. Either is good for poetry, but we cannot imagine them both being used in the same speech. And so, again and again, Mr. Lewis shows that his ear is untrue, or at least uncertain: sometimes he gives us the brisk up-to-date slangy note of Auden, and sometimes, within a few lines, the complex lofty language of Tennyson or Morris. Probably that is right for him, since he belongs to the generation which was reared on Victorian and Edwardian poetry and then went tight-lipped and modern; but it is not right for Vergil, who spent much time on creating a single, unique, unified style.

Both Lattimore's *Iliad* and Humphries' *Aeneid* are poetic translations. But some very interesting translations have been made in prose. Random House sells the *Iliad* and *Odyssey* in stately, archaic versions by Andrew Lang and three colleagues of his, they sound rather like the Bible and rather like Sir Thomas Malory. Samuel Butler put both poems into brisk matter-of-fact modern prose expressly to show that they were gripping stories with well-observed characters. More recently we have had translations by W. H. D. Rouse (New American Library) and E. V. Rieu (Penguin). These are the best translations to begin on. To begin on, but not to stay with. They show us the poems as wholes, stripped down and simplified. The story becomes clear. The colors become sharp and rather crude. Rouse was a jolly, extroverted English schoolmaster, and his translation is full of slang, which keeps something of the youthful energy and bursting animal spirits of Homer, but loses his dignity and his frequent grandeur. Rieu is less fanciful, and retells the tale as straightforward prose, which is always clear, but now and then a trifle dull. But they are both good to read. Homer—even when he is cruel and tragic—is always enjoyable, he makes you feel more fully alive; and that is the chief merit of Rouse and Rieu, that their translations move and live.

So much for epic poetry. What about translations of Greek drama? Here the problem seems to be much more serious, and translators have been less lucky. Gilbert Murray's renderings are sometimes very moving, but their Swinburnian cadences seem rather old-fashioned now. W. B. Yeats attempted the *Oedipus,* but he didn't really know enough Greek, and he was not temperamentally suited to the task. Some young contemporary poets have made valiant efforts to produce translations in the modern idiom, but seldom with complete success. At their best they remind me of the French prose translations of Shakespeare, and at their worst they are disastrous. I think the worst translation I have ever read is the *Agamemnon* as rendered by a normally competent poet and scholar, Louis MacNeice. Rex Warner has published versions of *Prometheus, Hippolytus,* and *Medea* in a style which avoids pomp and circumstance by going to the other extreme and becoming chatty and commonplace. In this country Dudley Fitts and Robert Fitzgerald have been working the same field for several years with more success. Their verses are nearly always poetically uplifting, although occasionally they stray too far from the Greek original.

Perhaps it is too early for us to expect really satisfying translations of Greek tragedy at this present stage. Perhaps the idiom and rhythms of modern poetic drama need to be more thoroughly explored, its powers and potentialities more closely tested, a new kind of rhetoric developed, before translators will have a suitable style at their disposal. The Athenians saw dozens and dozens of plays; their poets wrote and produced very copiously; they had a wide range of instruments to use. We seldom see a modern poetic play, and most of us feel that Eliot and Fry and others are still experimenting. When modern poetic drama is more firmly established, we can hope for richer translations of ancient drama.

Earlier we said that translation was a difficult art, and that it had been neglected; but that it had recently been more fully recognized and more skillfully practiced. We have had time to look at only one field; but in other areas there are many skillful translators with many striking successes to their credit. Scott-Moncrieff's equisite version of Proust is a masterpiece. Mrs. Lowe-Porter has grappled successfully with the fearful difficulties of Thomas Mann's thought and style. Justin O'Brien, in his magnificent four-volume translation of The *Journals of André Gide,* has produced not only a skillful rendering of Gide's spare and taut style, but a full critical apparatus without which the Journals would scarcely have been intelligible to the ordinary reader. Jacques Le Clercq has done the apparently impossible by both translating Rabelais and improving on the seventeenth-century translation by Urquhart and Motteux. There are many more among our contemporaries doing translations which do not merely serve as faithful reproductions of the original, but, written with genuine passion, with understanding, and with love, can very nearly claim to be original works. We do well to be grateful to such translators. They know we are blind and deaf, and they make it possible for us to see, and to hear.

———

Butcher and Lang, *Homer's Odyssey* (Random House, 1952).
C. Day Lewis, *Vergil's Aeneid* (Oxford, 1952).
R. Humphries, *Vergil's Aeneid* (Scribner, 1951).
Lang, Leaf, and Myers, *Homer's Iliad* (Random House, 1952).
R. Lattimore, *Homer's Iliad* (University of Chicago, 1951).
A. Manzoni, *The Betrothed* (tr. A. Colquhoun, Dutton, 1951).
E. V. Rieu, *Homer's Iliad* (Penguin, 1950).
W. H. D. Rouse, *Homer's Iliad* (Mentor Books, 1950).

The Pleasures of Satire

———————————

MY old friend, the Roman satirist Juvenal, says that when you look around at the corruptions and perversions of a big city 'it is difficult *not* to write satire.' But I think perhaps he is wrong. He took a long time preparing for his work: he studied the books of other satirists and the style of other poets with great care; he developed a fine technique and he chose important subjects. When you look at his poems, you realize that satire which is to mean something and last some time must be the result of long literary training, a firm grasp of the essential problems in life, and a rare blend of passion and control. Satire is just as valuable a type of writing as lyric poetry or fiction; but it is far harder to bring off. From time to time nowadays a prose satire is published—though very seldom; verse satire is practically a dead art. (I still hope, however, that Edmund Wilson will bring out a book of four or five satires in verse on the oddities of the Eastern States—he has already satirized the West Coast, bathed in suntan lotion and embalming fluid.)

In order to write satire of any kind, one has to have a number of special talents, and also a special attitude to the public. The talents are difficult enough to achieve, but it is even harder to reach the right relationship with one's readers. Of course, this is one aspect of the usual problem of writing. One has to develop one's own style, and make it into a means of communicating with one's invisible and speechless readers. They are there; one talks to them; but they hardly ever reply. In satire the problem is more complicated, for there the satirist's public are, almost by definition, either knaves and fools or the protectors of knaves and fools; and yet one has to bring them into sympathy with a denunciation of knavery and folly. Besides, the public usually does not believe that anything is deeply wrong with society, and it often thinks that a satirist is a sorehead. It has grown up and found a job and got married and brought up its children in the existing social framework. Why should it believe that the whole thing is tunneled through by gangsters, and bought and sold by crooked politicians, and redesigned to give the biggest profits to the ruthless and the corrupt? No, surely not. Therefore the satirist, who believes all these things, usually strains his voice shouting, to making the public hear; and then the public is even less inclined to listen.

We shall never expect satire to be a widely popular type of writing; and at present when so few of us care for poetry, we shall not expect any verse satire to take the minds of the public. The satirists of our own time seem to be rather special, writing on odd subjects and selling rather too few copies. No satire, of course, is written in totalitarian countries such as Hitler's Germany, and Russia, and Argentina: for satire is destructive criticism, and no totalitarian can stand that cold blast. You will ask what good is ever done by destructive criticism. The satirist will give no answer, except a loud raucous howl of laughter. But we may reply that its value is to remind people that we are all human. Even when men call themselves Caesar, or Commissar, or Voice of the Revolution; the First Earl, the Premier Duke, or the Blood Orange; the Central Secretary, the Indispensable Expert, or the Eminent Authority, they still have a strong chance of being pompous idiots or rat-minded crooks, and rather more temptation than most of us have, to be both at the same time. Hans Andersen once told a pretty story about an emperor who walked in a parade stark naked. No one liked to mention it until a child called out, 'Look, the emperor has no clothes on!' The satirist is an adult, not a child. He doesn't care whether the emperor is naked or clad: he simply calls out, 'Look, the emperor is a man like all the rest of us . . . and perhaps a little worse.'

Difficult as it is, satire has managed to produce several good practitioners in this generation—all in prose, of course, and nearly all in fiction. There are a number of non-fiction writers who have the impulse and the talent for satire. But usually they write too much, too often, and too indiscriminately. I am thinking of people like Robert Ruark and Westbrook Pegler, who feel they have to turn out a column every day five days a week—with the result that they spread their talents over many subjects of widely different importance, and diminish their effectiveness. Nothing worth while, nothing lasting, can be produced on a daily stint like that. Creation takes a long time.

The best satirist working in English is surely Evelyn Waugh. He is the son of a publisher, went to an inferior English 'public school' and a not very distinguished Oxford college, has now married a nobly born lady, and has appointed himself spokesman for the aristocracy; apparently conceiving himself as the son-in-law of a hundred earls. In America the most effective satirist is Mary McCarthy, who writes a peculiarly cold but skillful prose, as graceful as a deft surgical operation. There are a number of minor figures, equally eccentric: for instance, Nancy Mitford, a witty and excessively condescending member of one of the most eccentric British families; Aubrey Menen, who is half-Irish and half-Indian; and Philip Wylie, who will be good if he ever moves away from Florida.

It is rather tricky to distinguish satires from other types of book. Take a recent novelette by Louis Kronenberger called *Grand Right and Left*: a tale about a multibillionaire who has exhausted all the pleasures of life, and can see no reason for existing unless new pleasures are suggested. His wife (with his psychoanalyst) proposes that he should collect something unique and hitherto uncollected—namely, people. One of the people who is suggested first, as a specimen round whom the whole collection should be built, is of course Winston Churchill, and the billionaire is rather surprised that he refuses to become one of the exhibits. It is a pretty idea, isn't it? And yet it peters out. The rich man collects only four people altogether: a comic English peer, who talks the very reverse of English as she is spoke by English peers (really, Mr. Kronenberger, no one above the Lower Classes ever says 'Righty-o'!); a comic American authoress; and a suave French diplomat, with his 'niece.' And as you read the book you first become aware that it is not really a satire at all, since it does not attack anyone or anything; it is merely a fantasy. And then it is borne in upon you that it is not even a novel, but rather a three-act drawing-room comedy which Mr. Kronenberger has decided to publish as a novel, but which cannot conceal its origins, its light and symmetrical construction, its exits and entrances and its helpful butler, its limited cast, and even its Play within a Play. Comedy is not satire, though the two are cousins.

Or again, one might think that Graham Greene qualified as a satirist. Satirists hate most things; and Greene hates everything, including himself. (Somehow whenever I read him, I remember the story about the Boston lady who was driven through the slums by her nephew. The nephew said, 'Do you know, some of these houses have no heat and no running water!' The Boston lady said, 'Really, you would think they would have found out about that before moving in.') But seriously, is Greene a satirist? No, technically, he is not. He is something more like a tragedian; and tragedy is not satire either. A satirist can laugh, or at least sneer, at vice and folly. He does not pity and lament as Greene does. At the best, he laughs and cries, 'Lord, what fools these mortals be!' At the worst, he rages in a half-comic fury, or his lip curls in a snarl which is at least partly a bitter smile. Greene is always serious, and always sad.

The essence of satire is that people are silly and wicked, and that their silliness and wickedness are incongruous. One does not satirize sheer evil. It would be impossible to write a satire about the German crematoriums and the Russian prison camps. It might conceivably be possible to write a satire on the fantastic incongruity between the professed ideals of the German and the Russian one-party dictatorships and their brutal practice. In the center of Buchenwald, there stood that revered object, the oak of Goethe. The closest thing to such satire which we have had so far was Charlie Chaplin's splendid picture, *The Great Dictator*. Do you remember his badge, the Double Cross, and his bubble dance with the globe of the earth?

The essence of satire, then, is incongruity. And it needs a special talent to keep that in view while still feeling the blackness of vice and the flimsiness of folly. It is so much easier simply to denounce than to laugh. It needs an unusual gift of perception to see how wildly incongruous most of our everyday activities are, or how soon they can be reduced to utter nonsense by one twist of a wheel. Evelyn Waugh has one goodish satire called *Scoop.* It is about a press tycoon who calls for a feature writer to deal with a distant war. The wrong man is sent, a nature lover who has no idea of the trade of reporting. He blunders into a first-class story on the very day he is fired. Soon afterward, he is recalled, and happily returns to writing about Martha the Mole, and Matron Owl with her feathered brood, while the tycoon showers money and honors on the other man, the feature writer who should have gone out but who sat hopelessly at home because the press magnate had pushed the wrong button.

What Waugh likes best is the fearful prose of a logically compelled situation which follows a slight deviation from ordinary routine: the honeymoon couple, let us say, who step into the canoe just a hundred yards above Niagara Falls. In his *Black Mischief,* an African explorer takes part in a jolly feast with some friendly tribesmen; and only after it is over does he discover that the *pièce de résistance* was his sweetheart. In his best, *A Handful of Dust,* a similar explorer is detained in a remote Brazilian village, to read Dickens' novels out loud to an illiterate but inescapable chieftain, over and over and over again, for the rest of his natural life. (This prospect would terrify even Emlyn Williams.) In his funniest book, *The Loved One,* an attendant in a sumptuous California funeral parlor disposes of his own beloved, and arranges that his rival shall be sent a card every year on her deathday, on the same pattern as that which goes to the bereaved owners of little doggies. It says,

> Your little Aimée is wagging her tail in heaven tonight, thinking of you.

Mary McCarthy and an extremely sharp English satirist, Angus Wilson, have produced several good short stories on that kind of theme, the unbearable but inevitable sequence of events and thoughts which follows the initial false step. Sometimes one sees one's friends getting into these spirals, and it is pathetic but comic to watch. Sometimes one gets into them oneself, and finds them so fantastic that one can hardly bear to escape. (Perhaps the army is the supreme example of that. Do you know the story about the soldier who went into the bookstore? One of the salesgirls came up and said, 'Can I help you?' He said, 'Nobody can help me. I'm in the army.')

Miss McCarthy has also written some satiric novels; but in these she chooses situations which most people might consider rather unreal. *The Oasis* (1949) was about a Utopian colony, inhabited only by the sort of people who read and write for the Little Magazines: unreality squared, as it were. Her last, *The Groves of Academe,* deals with an almost equally odd group, the inhabitants of a small 'progressive' college. This tiny cosmos is torn apart by a great war. On one side there is a more than usually goofy teacher of literature who is devoted to James Joyce (and whose house smells nearly as awful as Joyce's novels); he is fired, and he resists his discharge on the ground that he was once a Communist and *therefore* ought not to be victimized. On the other side is a bluff extroverted pipe-smoking college president, who, finally, rather than be illiberal, rather than be a brutal Cossack . . . no, I must not tell you the outcome. You must read it, to get the full flavor of the satiric twist which might be called Mary McCarthyism.

They are very amusing and penetrating, these contemporary satires. The only trouble is this: they don't seem to matter much. Miss McCarthy spends a lot of care and observation on proving that the Dandelion League colleges are eccentric, confused, and hyper-emotional. Mr. Waugh exposes the burial ceremonies of the Californians with an odd blend of charm and callousness, like sweet-and-sour sauce. But such subjects are not terribly important. This, I regret to say, is the mid-twentieth century. What we need is a satirist bold enough to attack the crooks who run national politics in many countries; the parasites who make vast fortunes by buying something on Monday and selling it on Tuesday, usually to the government; the idealists who ship five million families off to labor camps in order to make their theories come right; the soreheads whose pride was hurt once and who are determined to start a war to take care of the bruise: the rats in the basement, the baboons playing with dynamite. Satire will not kill these animals; but it will make clear the difference between them and human beings, and perhaps inspire a human being to destroy them.

L. Kronenberger, *Grand Right and Left* (Viking, 1952).

M. McCarthy, *Groves of Academe* (Harcourt Brace, 1952).

M. McCarthy, *The Oasis* (Random House, 1949).

E. Waugh, *Black Mischief* (Little Brown, 1946).

E. Waugh, *A Handful of Dust* (Little Brown, 1944).

E. Waugh, *The Loved One* (Little Brown, 1948).

E. Waugh, *Scoop* (Little Brown, 1938).

Books and Cooks

———————

THE other day I was going through a bookseller's catalogue, and thinking of the enormous variety of human interests. This was not strictly a catalogue of books. It was a
catalogue of books about books—of bibliographies, listing the
most important or precious works on hundreds of different
subjects: bibliographies of armor, of Pennsylvania history, of
Charles Dickens, of cats. My eye was caught by one particular title, in German. Translated, it was this: *Two Thousand Years of Cookery.* It was a book about books about
cooks: a bibliography of gastronomy. I think it was the Two
Thousand Years that struck me; suddenly it made me realize
that cookery is an art, and an ancient and dignified art, too,
which amply deserves to be taken seriously and to have books
written about it.

To be taken seriously—not gloomily; for it is impossible to write sadly and somberly about cooking. People who have poor digestions usually shun the subject entirely. People who eat simply to fill up, people—if I may inject a small personal conviction—who eat hamburgers, usually think little or nothing of cookery and would never write or read about it. And there are very few people so opposed to cookery that they will write hostile and hateful books about it; although they do exist. Often they are vegetarians. They live on the bodies of murdered plants, on blackstrap molasses, and . . . nuts. The Russian Prince Paul Troubetzkoy almost ruined the taste of a distinguished modern gourmet by making him detest steak and mutton; he himself was an ardent, a violent vegetarian: and he wrecked many a dinner party by describing the soup as *jus cadavérique,* or corpse juice. Even worse, he was at luncheon once beside a charming French lady in a delicate condition. When he saw her eating a lamb chop, he was furious. Glaring at her plate and then glaring at her, he said, 'Madame, do you know that you are making your stomach into a cemetery?' She fainted, and disappeared beneath the luncheon table.

But such people are, fortunately, rare. Most of us enjoy eating; most of us enjoy talking about food; so many of us like books about cooking.

There are several different reasons for this. One is the amazing variety of the subject. In a single week, in New York, you can eat dozens of different dishes from all over the world, ranging through both geography and history. You can have Chinese almond chicken guy ding, with a sauce which may have been invented 2000 years ago; and Mexican enchiladas, which were devised by the Indians before the arrival of Columbus; and one of the kindliest inventions of the Pilgrim Mothers, beans baked with molasses; and a cherry soup from Hungary; and a glass of the wine which the Romans introduced into France, and ever since has been making glad the heart of man. Not all at the same meal, no, no; but certainly during the same week; and within the same forty or fifty blocks. Man is an ingenious and adaptable creature; his inventive powers have been shown in a thousand ways; and cookery is one of them.

Another reason for enjoying books on cooking is that cookery is a social art. It brings people together to share an enjoyable experience. The Greeks used to say that a man who ate alone was not eating, but feeding, like an animal; and certainly a dinner shared by six or eight people who like one another—or by two people who love each other—is a rich experience, enhancing both the pleasure of appetite and the joys of affection. Our own American festival, the Thanksgiving dinner, is a splendid example of that truth. (By the way, what do vegetarians eat on Thanksgiving Day? Roast cabbage?) So you will find that the reminiscences of distinguished gastronomes are seldom or never purely selfish. They are nearly always made up of stories about the delight of sharing several different but allied kinds of pleasure, which blend into something very like happiness.

But also, cookery is a matter of taste. And taste is highly individual. Therefore, books about eating and drinking are surprisingly varied. In half a dozen books on gastronomy you will find amazing differences of style, structure, material, and personality. A German once said 'Man ist, was man isst': what you eat, you are; and we might reverse it to say that *Cookery is character*. All great chefs and most gourmets have been individualists, with strong tempers and decided opinions, sometimes verging on violence. It would be inappropriate to recall all the stories about infuriated cooks brandishing kitchen knives, and enraged diners throwing plates on the floor; but I must recall one short and exquisite story about a poet who was also something of a gourmet. He was Walter Savage Landor: he was giving a luncheon in his villa in Florence: early springtime; his garden was just coming into bloom outside. But the main dish at luncheon was a failure. Landor summoned the cook, and upbraided him. The cook answered back, angrily. Landor seized him and threw him out of the window. And then, in agony, he cried, 'Oh heavens, I forgot the violets!'

There are hundreds, thousands of different dishes. And there are hundreds, thousands of different books about cooking. It is not very easy to describe them, because ultimately they become as complicated as the personalities of their writers. The most obvious and necessary type is the simple guide-book or encyclopedia, which assumes that the reader knows nothing and is anxious to learn. Two typical books of this kind are the standard American *Fanny Farmer's Cookbook*; and its French counterpart, *Tante Marie's French Kitchen,* translated and adapted by Charlotte Turgeon, herself a *cordon bleu* and wife of an eminent gastronomer. And the famous gourmet André Simon recently republished his *Encyclopaedia of Gastronomy,* a book which covers wine as well as food, and both of them with rich amplitude.

That encyclopedia by Simon merges into the second class, which is books of description. These tell us, for instance, where different kinds of cheese come from: how they are made, how they should be kept, served, and eaten. A good book of this kind has recently been put out, *The Holiday Book of Food and Drink,* by a collection of different authors including such eminent names as Lucius Beebe and Frank Schoonmaker. It ranges widely, from the invention of mustard flour to the biography of the St. Regis chef—a biography which also contains a good recipe for one of the finest folk dishes in Europe, *Cassoulet Toulousain.*

Even mentioning that splendid dish from Toulouse sets the mind traveling toward the paradise of epicures, southern France. And so there are many books of travel which center on cookery. An extremely funny set of such reminiscences came out in the fall of 1952: *Chef's Holiday,* by a man with a Welsh name, Idwal Jones. As it opens, a Parisian chef (whose family has cooked in the same house for a hundred years) determines to leave for a short vacation in Brittany. As a chef, he knows just where to go to eat well; somehow he is connected with a traveling circus, which insures variety and adds another kind of enjoyment; and all along the way he finds not only local variations of cooking, but individual masterpieces, created by poets of the saucepan and artists of the casserole. Some of the best gastronomical reminiscences I have read occur in the work of an American lady, who unfortunately does not seem to have been publishing recently. Her name is M. F. K. Fisher; and I particularly enjoyed two books of hers called *How to Cook a Wolf* and *The Gastronomical Me,* produced about ten years ago. (Miss Fisher has traveled a great deal: she spent about three years in Dijon, one of the food-and-wine capitals of the entire world, and three years more in western Switzerland, near Vevey, where both food and drink are delicate and delicious.) Her work is almost too emotional sometimes; but cookery is an emotional art.

This kind of book easily leads to the highest type of gastronomical work: the book of meditations, the philosophical essays in which a happy man talks partly to us and partly to himself about one of the secrets of happiness. The best of such books are calm, judicious, and serene; fastidious, too, for choice and rejection are essential to good eating; but essentially positive. To live is a chemical process; but to live well is a matter of thought and taste—and that is true of choosing a meal no less than of choosing a house or a wife. Such works, however, are rare. I have just been reading an attempt at one which, unhappily, is a partial failure, because the author does not write well enough. Perhaps he really thinks in another language: and if so, his book has been inadequately translated. (For instance, take this sentence from a description of the famous seafood restaurant, Prunier's in Paris:

> More like a fish mart than a restaurant is its façade, whose windows are a field of ice upon which outstretched finny beauties tempt.

Surely a bad translation; or perhaps the oven wasn't right.) And yet the book is full of good ideas and pleasant stories: it is called *Candlelight and Cookery,* by Carlos de Florez. The tale about the vegetarian Prince Troubetzkoy comes from this book, and there are dozens of others . . . (Only the other day I heard one from a visitor to Peiping before the Communists took over: he was entertained at an old and famous restaurant, which had a large poster outside. He asked what the poster meant, and was told it said UNDER NEW MANAGEMENT. His Chinese hosts asked the proprietor when the change was made: he said, 'About 200 years ago.')

The classic of all such books is *The Physiology of Taste,* by Anthelme Brillat-Savarin, which was published in 1825, and was translated into English 100 years later by Arthur Machen (Boni and Liveright published the translation here in 1926). The author was a lawyer, who was too moderate for the French revolutionaries and had to emigrate: first to Switzerland, and then to New York, where he taught French, played in an orchestra, and sampled the local dishes. In 1796 he returned to Paris, became a judge, and survived to eat and meditate for a quarter of a century—at the end of which he produced the finest book of its kind in the Western world. It is composed of thirty Meditations, which would be mystical if they were not so closely attached to this life; and twenty-six short chapters of Varieties, a sort of dessert of reminiscences. The Meditations are the heart of the book: or the main dishes of the dinner. They cover history, chemistry, biology, wit, and social graces; and they are full of delightful personal reminiscences. There is one about Brillat-Savarin, a wild turkey, and some partridges in what he calls a 'virgin forest' just outside 'Harfort,' in Connecticut: he himself roasted the turkey, and, before it, served partridge wings *en papillote*.

The reality and common sense of *The Physiology of Taste* are shown by one fact. Meditations xxi and xxii deal with subjects which most gourmands rarely mention but often think of: obesity; overweight; in fact, fat. Brillat-Savarin was a great big powerful fellow, and he managed to look majestic, but not sloppy. He himself writes:

> I have always considered my belly as a formidable enemy; I have conquered it, but the struggle between us has lasted for 30 years.

In order to do this, he had to adopt certain sound principles. He would not touch potatoes, or leguminous vegetables like beans, or starches; nor would he lie late in the morning, for he realized that long sleep may improve the health, but it rounds out the figure; and in his xxiind Meditation he preaches gravely and wisely to those who would like to eat well without becoming obese and unhealthy. His counsels are difficult to follow; but then, all art is difficult, and gastronomy is an art. It is one of the arts which make up the chief art of all: the art of living.

A. Brillat-Savarin, *Physiologie du goût* (Charpentier, Paris, 1865; tr. A. Machen, Boni & Liveright, 1926).

Fanny Farmer's Cookbook (ed. W. Perkins, Little Brown, 1946).

M. F. K. Fisher, *The Gastronomical Me* (Duell, Sloan, & Pearce, 1943).

M. F. K. Fisher, *Here Let Us Feast* (Viking, 1946).

M. F. K. Fisher, *How to Cook a Wolf* (Duell, Sloan & Pearce, 1942).

C. de Florez, *Candlelight and Cookery* (Bond Wheelwright, 1952).

Holiday Book of Food and Drink (Hermitage House, 1952).

I. Jones, *Chef's Holiday* (Longmans, Green, 1952).

Tante Marie's French Kitchen (tr. and ed. C. Turgeon, Oxford, 1949).

A. Simon, *Concise Encyclopaedia of Gastronomy* (Harcourt Brace, 1952).

The Sense of Nonsense: Dada and Surrealism

ON the whole, the world of art, and literature, and thought is an orderly world. The symphony and the tragedy are carefully constructed, like gigantic engines; the picture is elaborately composed, with lines, planes, and colors all supporting and enhancing one another; most novels and histories are built like inhabitable houses. Yes, that world is usually orderly, and one of the chief reasons we admire it is that it introduces a higher kind of order into what sometimes seems to be a mere succession of dismally trivial events, our daily life.

But *need* it be orderly? Can art be trivial, and ridiculous? Can it be as petty as our everyday existence? Should we call it art, if it were?

I don't know if you have ever looked at a page of a newspaper as you would look at a work of art: it is an instructive experience. At the top you see three stories from three different parts of the country, one about a dog in Michigan which pushed a child out of the way of a rolling car; one about a man in Louisiana who has married for the seventeenth time; and one about a flash flood in California. Then there is a gigantic announcement about a new line of garbage disposer; TRY IT FOR ONE WEEK, the page shouts at you in the unsubtle but memorable accents of advertising: NO MORE KITCHEN SMELLS. Beneath that two smaller announcements about quick-frying fat and quick-freezing stomachs; and then one of those things called 'fillers,' which finish off a page without any blank space—except in the mind of the reader who has just been informed that

The salmon often swims 800 miles in order to spawn

or

The University of San Marcos in Lima is the oldest in the Western Hemisphere.

This is the sort of thing that people read every day. Why should art not sometimes be like that? or always? Have you ever watched a man doodling on a piece of paper? He seldom or never creates a logical work of art; but nearly always makes random patterns with no ulterior meaning and little central plan. Can art be created on that almost total absence of purpose?

Recently there have been two movements which thought that it could. One was Dada. The other was, and is, Surrealism. I have been interested in them for many years, and recently I have been thinking about them a little harder, for two reasons. One reason is that I have been trying to reassess my own job, the literature that I deal with. Usually the Greek and Roman authors are conceived as powerful thinkers, but cool, calm, cold, almost petrified. I have lately been asking myself if this is not a Victorian or a baroque mistake, and if they are not in fact extremely emotional writers who owe their success to the tremendous charge of feeling they put into their books and to the precariousness of its control by their powerful intellectual and stylistic standards. If these people kept doing their best to grapple with disruptive forces in society and in the soul, then to study them would also throw much more light on such modern writers as Dostoevsky and Kafka, who are hard to understand, but who were involved in the same conflict. The second reason for my interest is the appearance of a large anthology, the biggest and most complete to date, of *The Dada Painters and Poets,* edited by Robert Motherwell.

(I already possessed Georges Lemaître's *From Cubism to Surrealism in French Literature,* two books on Surrealism published in the 'thirties by David Gascoyne and Herbert Read, and Alfred Barr's splendid catalogue of the Museum of Modern Art's exhibition of Fantastic Art in 1936.)

Let us look at these two movements . . . or, more exactly, these two processes of the same movement. What are they?

Dada means geegee, the child's name for a horse in French. The name was chosen by accident, we are told; and yet it is appropriate, for it is more a pair of nonsense syllables than a name; and it is used by children, who (the Dadaists thought) know more than adults. The movement was founded in Zurich in 1916 by a group of odd characters who had come to Switzerland to escape the war. In due course it moved to Paris and to Germany, but the Parisian section was far more vocal and successful. About 1922 it broke up in the usual factionalism which plagues French art almost as much as French politics. Its principles were: nonsense; the fist in the face; directness; hatred of art as a thing meant for drawing rooms and museums; scorn of social conventions (remember, its members were suffering from the impact of the First World War, which seemed to them to imply that progress and religion and patriotism and science were all aimed at producing bloodshed and corruption); scorn of the intellect and of logic; reverence for excitement, irrational emotion, unjustifiable acts; and, with all this, a strong vein of humor which was sometimes disgusting, sometimes macabre, and sometimes quite charming, with the crazy charm of a student's joke.

Surrealism is a bad transliteration of the French, and ought to have been Super-Realism, meaning *a higher form of realism*. The word was coined in 1917 by the French-Polish-Italian screwball Guillaume Apollinaire, and adopted by André Breton and the others in 1924 or earlier. The movement itself had been brewing for a long time, much longer than Dada, and it had many predecessors in nineteenth-century literature, men like Rimbaud and Lautréamont; but its principles were not laid down coherently until the decade after the First War. It is a much more important thing than Dada. Its chief principle is one which may well be profoundly true, and which has been set forth by many men working in quite different fields: namely, that the subconscious is more creative than the conscious. In particular, our most important ideas are sent up, are created without deliberate effort, by the subconscious. All that the conscious mind can do is to shape and control them, too often to deform them and ruin them. The world of the imagination is the super-reality for all of us, not only for children and artists, but for people who, if interrogated, would say that they were stern realists, devoted to facts.

There is a famous essay on Kansas by the late Carl Becker which brings this out. He says that 'every Kansan wishes first of all to tell you that he comes from the town of X, and then that it is the finest town in the State.' When the town is described as it actually is, it turns out to be rather plain and dreary, hot and thirsty and dusty. But, says Becker, you at last discover the secret of his enthusiasm in the inevitable 'it will be a great country some day,' and it dawns upon you that, after all, the man does not live in the dreary town of X, but in the great country of SOME DAY.

You wouldn't think one could describe a Kansas merchant as a Surrealist, would you? But I believe that you can, and I believe that the Surrealists have got hold of an important positive truth, far more useful than the destructive violences of the Dadaists.

I think the Surrealists would go further, and say—along with many doctors—that much of our unhappiness comes from our attempt to make everything real and rational, our refusal to admit that we inhabit two worlds and that we should let them interpenetrate to get the best out of them both. Love does that for us. Shakespeare said,

> The lunatic, the lover, and the poet
> Are of imagination all compact;

and others, such as Havelock Ellis, have told us that love can be not only a temporary intoxication but a permanent super-reality transfiguring our whole workaday existence. For some of the Surrealists an apparently random set of images, things seen by accident, chance juxtapositions of diverse objects, will assume a magical power and dominate part of their lives for a long time. Sometimes a dream, an impossible vision, can haunt a man so awakened and shape his thought and imagination most powerfully. Salvador Dali is the best example of this. Lately, like many of his generation, he has been feeling a strong pull toward religion, and has created several very devout paintings which contrast oddly with the obscenities of some of his earlier work. Now, one of the impossibilities which first haunted him was the idea that, instead of being more or less solid, the human body might be collapsible, or extensible, or partly displaceable: he did drawings of people who had sets of drawers sliding in and out of their torsos, and a painting of his old nurse sitting on the shore, with a cubical section taken right out of her back, so that the beach and the sea were visible between her shoulderblades. So far, this is merely fanciful: it is not hopeless nonsense, for you remember these pictures after you have seen them; but it does not say much. However, a year or two ago he did a very elaborate painting of the Madonna and Child, *The Madonna of Port Lligat*; the Child was a beautiful little boy of about two, floating above his mother's lap. The same piece of magic appears in this work; but now it has meaning. In the center of the Child's body there is a transparent gap, like a reliquary; and in the center of that there floats a piece of bread: the Eucharist.

The question is whether these two movements, Dada and Surrealism, have produced any results which will last, any works of art which matter and will continue to matter.

Dada, I think, produced none. It was merely negative. It was a bomb bursting. It destroyed a lot (how much it destroyed one can hardly realize until one reconstructs the popular taste of the years 1906-16) and rearranged a lot of fragments and cleared some ground. Paul Klee and Chirico and other artists of that caliber had been producing before Dada was founded and went on, or else matured, after it died, although they sympathized with the movement during its brief existence. What will chiefly be remembered from Dada is a series of large and outrageous jokes: the exhibition at which visitors were given an axe to destroy any works of art they disliked, Marcel Duchamp's picture of the Mona Lisa with a beard and moustache added, and the goofy lives —and even names—of people like Tzara and Schwitters.

Surrealism, on the other hand, has already produced a great deal of good painting and sculpture, several distinguished movies. (Of course we cannot limit the movement to the few who officially accepted André Breton's leadership: we must consider it as a broad current of the spirit, like Romanticism a century or so earlier. On that basis Cocteau's wonderful film, *Beauty and the Beast,* is a Surrealist masterpiece.) Yves Tanguy, now working in this country, has painted a number of really lovely poetic pictures of a never-never land, which might be the shores of a sea, never visited by human beings but inhabited by benign and decorative plants and animals unlike those of our world. Dali is an important artist, of the same rank as Magnasco, and is still growing. Joan Miró does huge decorative paintings which are charming until you notice how brutal and naughty they often are. The Chilean artist Matta depicts scenes almost as terrifying as those of recent reality. Picasso contains Surrealism, as he contains so much else.

But apart from the plastic arts, Surrealism strictly defined has so far produced little of interest. Perhaps this is because its writers have misconceived their method. They have too often thought that their words and images should be set shapelessly down, just as they were 'given'; while in fact, even when incoherent or illogical, they need to be constructed as a painting is constructed. Surrealism in fact is a recent version of a much older attitude to the world, which has been practiced by many skillful writers and artists. *Alice in Wonderland* is a Surrealist book; 'Jabberwocky' is a splendid Surrealist poem; The Revelation of St. John is a wonderful

Surrealist book, and 'The Ancient Mariner' almost wholly a Surrealist poem. André Breton, the self-elected leader of the Surrealists, was never a very interesting writer, and he showed his misunderstanding of the whole thing by converting it into a propaganda organ for one single political creed. The liberation of the imagination and the assertion of the individual can have nothing to do with the dictatorship of a single monolithic party. But, knowing the French, we may surely expect a new leader to appear, shouting:

SURREALISTS OF THE WORLD, ARISE!
YOU HAVE NOTHING TO LOSE BUT YOUR BRAINS!

A. Barr (ed.), *Fantastic Art, Dada, Surrealism* (Museum of Modern Art, 1936).

C. Becker, *Everyman His Own Historian* (Appleton-Century-Crofts, 1948).

D. Gascoyne, *A Short Survey of Surrealism* (Cobden-Sanderson, London, 1935).

G. Lemaître, *From Cubism to Surrealism in French Literature* (Harvard University Press, 1947).

R. Motherwell (ed.), *The Dada Painters and Poets* (Wittenborn, Schultz, 1951).

H. Read (ed.), *Surrealism* (Harcourt Brace, 1937).

The Case of the Disappearing Detectives

—————————

SOME months ago I was at a party in one of the three most beautiful cities in America, and the city with the most peculiar, willful, and exasperating climate. (Yes, you have guessed it: San Francisco.) Most of the guests turned out to be people interested in the arts. After a while, I fell into conversation with a group of pleasant people, who had a lively flow of rather eccentric conversation, a strong sense of humor, and a fund of unusual information. Obviously they enjoyed life. But after some time, they grew serious. They began to talk about their profession. They all turned out to be mystery-story writers. They were quite proud of it: yet they spoke of it with a certain melancholy. At first, as writers do, they complained a bit about publishers, saying that their work was poorly paid and badly advertised. But then they went on to say that what really hurt them most was neglect —a neglect which they felt was something very close to contempt. Serious critics, they complained, never reviewed a detective story however carefully it was written. In the important reviews like the Sunday *New York Times,* there was always (they said) a separate ghetto for 'mysteries' away at the back; and monthly magazines and journals of opinion never deigned to mention detective stories at all.

My friends went on, warming up to their subject. Why, they said, even in libraries you will notice that our side of the writing profession is neglected. Trashy historical novels, in which the clash of important forces and the interplay of famous personalities has been reduced to a few duels, seductions, and torture scenes; eccentric regional stories written in an almost unintelligible dialect, chronicling the feuds and follies of a few families in a district as remote and improbable as Dogpatch—these, and others like them, are classified as Serious Fiction. But detective stories on which just as much research and care have been expended are not purchased at all by the big permanent libraries; and in the lending libraries, they are placed in a side alcove, with Max Brand on one side and the Rocket-Ship Rovers on the other. Don't you think (they said) that this is rather hard—particularly since lots of people do read us? We have our public; we get letters from many sensible and intelligent men and women who are enthusiastic collectors of our work, who criticize our books carefully, and who look forward to the next. Why are we not taken seriously?

I couldn't answer the question right away; and at that moment someone put on a new set of records of Gieseking playing Debussy; and the party finally broke up leaving the discussion unfinished. But afterward, driving home through the thick, swirling ocean fog which is San Francisco's Midsummer-Nightmare, I kept thinking about the subject, and wondering whether these pleasant fellows had any right to complain, or not. I have been thinking about it ever since.

Certainly they had not understated their case. Lots of people read mysteries, but hardly anyone seems to take them as seriously as a regular novel. Publishers usually sell them more cheaply and don't bind and print them so well. Whenever serious critics take notice of the detective story, it is nearly always to abuse it. Seven or eight years ago Edmund Wilson wrote three devastating essays on the vapidity, the artificiality, and the intellectual vulgarity of the mystery story: you will find them in his *Classics and Commercials,* and they are well worth reading. And an unexpected blow was administered a few years earlier by one of the best living detective-story writers, Raymond Chandler, who turned on the profession as a whole, and said that most of its products were bogus unrealistic trash. See his essay, 'The Simple Art of Murder.' This, as Mark Antony said, this was the most unkindest cut of all.

And yet, you know, in spite of all this, there must be something valuable about detective stories. To begin with, they do correspond to a real phase of contemporary life. There is a great deal of crime in the daily papers. It runs third to politics and sport, and sometimes gets mixed up with both of them. There is a great deal of discussion of crime in serious magazines; it is debated by important civic bodies; it has made its way into big business and into labor unions, it is invading national defense and infecting national politics; it is a vital issue. Therefore, surely a book about crime and its detection deals with an urgent and absorbing topic: it *ought* to command our serious interest.

Then again, it cannot be doubted that mystery stories give pleasure to many intelligent people. As my friends in San Francisco told me, those who read detective stories and write to their authors usually show keen perception and command a wide range of knowledge. Most of us have known or heard of distinguished men of high intellectual caliber, who habitually read mysteries in preference to any other kind of fiction. Professor J. A. Smith of Oxford, who knew about fifty languages and was a remarkably keen metaphysician, had a library of many hundreds of detective stories; so had Paul Elmer More of Princeton; quite a number of intellectuals not only read them but write them—Michael Innes is a don at Oxford, John August is an eminent American critic.

And yet, there is something wrong with them. There is something wrong with the complex relationship between the writers, and their subjects, and their style, and their public, and the society in which they live, and the rest of literature.

There is one strong piece of evidence. This is THE CURIOUS INCIDENT OF THE DISAPPEARING DETECTIVES.

The best writers in the field have all been able to create original and memorable detectives to solve their mysteries. But nearly always these characters either die suddenly, or else vanish into the limbo of unreality.

Sometimes the detective solves a few cases brilliantly; and then drops completely out of sight. The author abruptly abolishes him. The first great detective in modern fiction was Edgar Allan Poe's Auguste Dupin. He solved three remarkable cases (*The Murders in the Rue Morgue, The Mystery of Marie Rogêt,* and *The Purloined Letter*). Then he vanished. (I know what happened to him: he took up writing, and some years later he published a book of poems called *Les Fleurs du mal*; but he retired from detective work forever.) Then in England, more recently, some have lamented the disappearance of Lord Peter Wimsey. In this country two eminent detectives projected by Dashiell Hammett showed up for only a few cases and then melted away: they were

Sam Spade (remember Bogart as Spade in *The Maltese Falcon?*) and Nick Charles of *The Thin Man*. And what happened to the Private Eye of Raymond Chandler, who still gets reprinted but seldom appears in a new story? Of course we all remember the most dramatic disappearance of all, the murder of Sherlock Holmes. Conan Doyle disguised himself as an Irish professor, and pushed Holmes over a precipice.

Poor Sherlock Holmes! He suffered *both* the fates of the fictional detective. First, he was killed by his creator. And then, brought back to life, he endured the second fate, which is to fade away into senility, garrulity, and repetition. The shock of his zombie-like resurrection was too much for him, his brain was already weakened by drugs, and at last, like a figure in a Kafka story, he found himself reliving his earlier adventures *without remembering them*. (To give only one example, in 1902 he solved the case of *The Three Garridebs* without seeing that it was on exactly the same pattern as his triumph in 1890 over *The Red-Headed League*.)

The same thing happens to other detectives. Think of Erle Stanley Gardner's unfortunate Perry Mason. He has been going on and on for years. Any normal man would have retired, or been disbarred, or stepped out to run for Lieutenant-Governor. But Mason goes on hiding witnesses and trusting Della Street with a compulsive repetitiveness which shows that his mind is going. Something of the same kind has happened to the British Home Office expert, Mr. Fortune. His first fifteen or twenty cases were really brilliant; and his own plump epicurean personality was delightful; but he has become more and more slangy, and the other characters more and more cryptically English, and the detection less and less convincing, until now Fortune is in disgrace with men's eyes.

Now, the fact that so many detectives either die suddenly,

or else go on repeating themselves more and more faintly—like figures seen in a row of mirrors—tells us one of the things that is wrong with the mystery story. It is this. The mystery story pretends to be realistic; but the character of the detective is usually unreal. In life, detective work is painfully complicated, takes a lot of learning, and is a full-time career. But hardly any of the fictional detectives ever builds one case upon another and follows an authentic career-pattern, moving up as people do in the police, in the FBI and Scotland Yard, or in Pinkerton's Agency. Real detectives use their experience. After they have seen seventy or eighty cases of embezzlement or murder, they begin to know the patterns. They say, 'now, this setup here is very like that 1933 job: that was the brother-in-law, I remember, so let's see if he is involved here.' But fictional detectives seldom do this. I believe that is because their authors dare not presume that anyone who picks up a new story about a detective will remember reading about the same detective before, and put one and one together.

There are a few praiseworthy exceptions. Rex Stout's detective Nero Wolfe does change from story to story; he and his legman Archie Goodwin have a living career and developing personalities. Michael Innes's hero Appleby began, I think, simply as a metropolitan policeman: he rose through case after case, got married to a handsome sculptress he met in one of his adventures, and is now rather grand, an Assistant Commissioner or something of the kind. And let us never forget the admirably real Inspector Maigret, created by Simenon. These and a few others live; but most fictional detectives do not live; they merely pop up again and again, in a series of quite unrelated cases.

Then again, we must admit that the writing of too many detective stories is bad. It is careless and slipshod, either full of painful affectations like those deadly things about Philo

Vance, or marred by errors in syntax and style which come from rapid writing and superficial editing, or padded with long unimportant conversations, or exaggerated with wildly improbable boozing and brutalizing. It looks as though most of them expected to be read only once and then thrown away. Books which make no more claim than that cannot pretend to be literature.

Raymond Chandler has pointed out another defect in many of them. It is that the methods of fictional detectives are bogus. For instance, all real detective agencies use informers, and keep the best ones permanently on their payroll; but informers seldom appear in fiction. Again, one of the best methods of getting information out of a suspect is to interrogate him for hours and hours . . . not a third degree, not the Russian method of torture and exhaustion and drugging; no, giving him ample time for rest and food and reflection; but simply going on and on with the interrogation until the story *either* develops so many connections with established fact that it must be true *or else* hardens into an obviously artificial creation full of gaps and discrepancies, which the suspect repeats mechanically and cannot explain. (Two recent books about real-life detection show this. One is Oreste Pinto's *Spy Catcher* (Harper), which contains a good introduction on methods of interrogation, emphasizing patience. The other is Alan Moorehead's *The Traitors* (Scribner), in which you ought to read the leisurely and polite process, without threats or compulsions, by which a security officer finally extracted the truth from Dr. Klaus Fuchs.) But fictional detectives seldom or never conduct such interrogations —with one great exception, the magistrate Porphyry.

Not long ago, a contemporary American playwright began to feel this, too. He realized that crime and detection made a fascinating subject; but he thought that its real meaning was misrepresented by melodrama on the movies and TV and by *The Case of the Blackened Bananas* in fiction. So he spent more than a year in the company of real policemen and real detectives, listening to the run of business, talking to the officers, observing not only their methods but their relation to the public. For a month, he was virtually a member of the homicide squad in a big American city, on call twenty-four hours a day. After that, he wrote his experience and observations into a fine play. His name is Sidney Kingsley, and the play is called simply *Detective Story*. It is tragic. It is real.

Surely that is the point. That is what most mystery-story writers leave out—because they are too closely occupied with the mechanics of their puzzle; because they are afraid to ask too much of their public; because sometimes they have no close experience of real police work; sometimes because they have not thought long enough about human character; sometimes because they are trying to write two different kinds of book at once. Crime is a powerful chemistry. A murder, a blackmailing operation, a kidnapping, a big robbery actually changes the personalities of all those who are involved. It induces an interplay of character on quite new levels, and at unprecedented intensities. The ultimate subject of all stories about serious crime and mystery and detection is the one which most of their authors leave out: the social forces and the spiritual transformations which are set in motion by a single violent or cunning act, and which are intensified by the whole process of detection. Crime is a tragic subject. Most mystery stories are comic. They have a light touch, and a happy ending.

Therefore, almost the only stories of crime and detection which can claim to be satisfactory literature are those which embody the tragedy that accompanies crime. (The only exceptions would be the comparatively rare mysteries which deal with fraud, robbery, and trickery in general: they are legitimately comic and romantic.) We find this tragic sense in Sidney Kingsley's play; in Simenon; in one or two other mystery writers, like Mabel Seeley; and in an occasional film made by a gifted psychologist like Hitchcock. On a higher level, the best mysteries today are being written by two serious novelists, Graham Greene and William Faulkner. On a higher level still are two great books: one in French, *Les Misérables*; the other—and still champion—the Russian masterpiece *Crime and Punishment*. It is really a mistake for mystery writers to form a special clique, and to address a special audience. Their whole subject is the oldest subject in the world. As such, it demands the whole effort of both the author and the reader, working together, to make and appreciate a book worthy of that supreme mystery, the human soul, fatally and tragically enmeshed in its sins and the atonement for them.

R. Chandler, *The Simple Art of Murder* (Houghton Mifflin, 1950).

D. Hammett, *The Maltese Falcon* (Knopf, 1945).

D. Hammett, *The Thin Man* (Knopf, 1934).

S. Kingsley, *Detective Story* (Random House, 1949).

E. Wilson, *Classics and Commercials* (Farrar, Straus, 1950).

Prison Books

ONE of the finest books in the world was written in a
condemned cell, some 1400 years ago. That was in the early
Dark Ages. Roman civilization still existed, more or less; but
there was no more Roman state in the West—something much
worse, something primitive and scarcely rational, a lot of
warring barbarian kingdoms. Italy was ruled by the Ostro-
goths under their king Theodoric. One of the last fully civil-
ized minds still existing belonged to a Roman statesman and
scholar called Boethius. When he was about 40, he was arrested, on the charge of treason to the barbarian government,
thrown into a solitary dungeon, and after some time executed
with crude and savage tortures.

But before he died he wrote a book which was read, and
reread, and translated into many languages, for over 1000
years. He called it *The Consolation of Philosophy*. It opens
with a description of himself in prison—ruined, lonely, and

hopeless. In his despair he tries to comfort himself by remembering and composing poetry, but it is useless. He collapses. He weeps. His life has stopped, and he feels he is simply a corpse waiting to die. But at this crisis a stately Lady appears in his cell, and begins to talk to him. He tells her of his agony. She replies that he is sick; he is mentally ill; he has forgotten the true meaning and purpose of human life, in which the explanation of such suffering and the cure for such despair are contained. And she starts, in a series of slow, kindly, wise conversations, to teach him and to cure him.

The book is one of the great educational works of the western world, for it shows us how a sick soul can be cured by a conversation with—Philosophy? No, with itself. It gives deeply thought-out answers to many of the crucial problems of suffering; and as we read it, not only do we see Boethius himself being cured, but we ourselves are educated and strengthened.

That was *The Consolation of Philosophy*, by Boethius: one of Dante's favorite books, it consoled him in his bereavement; it cheered King Alfred surrounded by the savage Danes; it was translated into English by Alfred, by Chaucer, and by another great prisoner, Queen Elizabeth I. It is one of the first of a special class of books which forms a separate section in every thoughtful man's library, and which has been rapidly growing during our own generation. These are Prison Books—books written in prison by men who never got out, or about prison by men and friends of men who finally escaped or were released. They make painful reading; and yet it is necessary reading; nearly always it is uplifting, in a terrible sort of way.

When you are a prisoner, there are three things you can do. You can escape; or you can stay in prison and fight to keep your spiritual freedom; or you can give in. Most of those who collapsed in the German concentration camps formed a peculiar group, with a peculiar slang name. They were called Moslems, because they had given in. They had become complete fatalists, passively living instead of acting. Others give in by confessing and accepting the will of their jailers; or else join the prison authorities and collaborate, so that technically they cease to be prisoners.

About escape, there are a number of first-rate books, both fictional and factual. It does not much matter which, because, in this field, truth usually rivals fiction and often outdoes it. You might think that the most melodramatic and improbable story of escape was Alexandre Dumas' *The Count of Monte Cristo,* in which a 'lifer' gets out by substituting himself for a corpse in a neighboring cell, and then, sewn into a sack, is thrown off a cliff into the sea. But the true stories are even more fantastic and far more complicated. I remember a story from the First World War called *The Road to En-Dor.* Here a group of British officers held prisoner in Turkey developed their abilities as conjurers and tricksters. Then they persuaded the camp commandant that, through table-turning and an ouija board, they were in touch with the Unseen; and that they had located a vast hidden treasure some miles away from the camp, which they could find and share under guidance from the spirits. This got them out of the camp, and eventually out of Turkey altogether.

A good escape book by E. E. Williams, called *The Wooden Horse,* was made into a fine movie. Here a similar group determined to dig a tunnel out of a military prison. The difficulty was that the huts were raised, so that they could hardly work through the floor. So they got permission to build a vaulting-horse for gymnastic exercises. Every day they carried this thing out to the center of the exercise ground, put it down, and spent hours and hours vaulting over it, indulgently watched by the guards: while the digger who had been secreted inside it opened up the tunnel mouth concealed below, excavated some more cubic feet of earth, lugged it back into the horse, and was carried back to the huts again at sunset, earth and all.

An even more fantastic story is told by Paul Brickhill in *The Great Escape*. In this a group of Allied officers worked for many months to construct an underground tunnel which actually had a subway train running along it on ropes, with an air pump and electric light. They also made 250 compasses, 50 complete suits of clothes, and 400 forged papers. No less than 76 of them escaped all at once. (Hitler ordered that over half of those recaptured should be shot, so that 50 of them died; but their murderers were caught, tried and hanged.) Although that story ended tragically, the actual planning of the escape was very gay. Once when a German general came down in his car to inspect the camp, they stole his flashlight, map case, gloves, and car tools, as well as a secret German Army handbook, which they later returned to the commandant stamped *Passed by British Censor*.

The R.A.F. were great escapers. They could not bear to be shut up inside a fence, whereas quite a lot of infantrymen got accustomed to it—perhaps because they knew more about walking. After the war was over they actually formed a Royal Air Force Escaping Society, whose principal object is to express the gratitude of its members to those gallant men, women, and sometimes children, who helped the R.A.F. prisoners to get away. Eight of the most dramatic stories of these escapes are told, or edited, by Paul Brickhill in *Escape or Die*. They are all exciting, all uplifting, and sometimes terrible: McCormac's escape from Japanese torturers, through the jungles of Malaya, is worth an entire book by itself.

The most delightful of all such stories, for my money, is still Casanova's escape from his cell in the Doge's prison in Venice. His problem was an unusual one, for he was up under the roof, and so had to escape sideways and downward. He himself refused to tell the story in less than an hour and a half, and I shall not insult his memory by summarizing it. (It would be difficult in any case to insult Casanova's memory.) This tale, and nearly thirty others, are told as nearly as possible in the words of the escapers in a fine anthology called *Great Escapes,* edited by Basil Davenport. The most phenomenal of all these, perhaps, is the escape of a New England seaman from the belly of a whale. But no, they are all phenomenal.

But what of those who cannot escape? Like Boethius, they must endure, and try to keep their own selves free. There are many painful books, and more are constantly appearing, about the strange and tormenting processes of strengthening and conversion which go on in the human soul under imprisonment. Oscar Wilde's 'Ballad of Reading Gaol' is the result of such meditations; and so is Dostoevsky's *House of the Dead.* I admit I do not fully understand Dostoevsky's character; but *The House of the Dead* looks to me like an early example of that peculiar Russian phenomenon, the conversion of a prisoner to the admission of his own guilt. Dostoevsky did not feel that those who imprisoned him and exiled him were proving themselves wrong. He came to believe that, because he was in prison, he must be guilty; and when he emerged, he was on their side. Another such work is Arthur Koestler's *Darkness at Noon,* although there the *full* Russian technique of extorting confession is employed. But in Italian there is a classic of resistance, Silvio Péllico's book *My Prisons.* Péllico was imprisoned by the Austrians who ruled Italy a century or so ago, and kept for about seven years in solitary confinement and chains; but he retained his loftiness of character, his idealism, and his sanity, largely by reading the Bible and by reflections, some of which he wrote down to strengthen his mind and assure himself that it was still working logically.

When torture is added to imprisonment, then the problem of survival, both physical and spiritual, becomes far more difficult. Strange—when I was at school, torture was a thing one heard of only in books about the Middle Ages, or China, or the Red Indians; one assumed that Progress had rendered it obsolete in the Western world; and now book after book has come out, by men who have endured it and outlived it. A century ago, an American author wrote an immortal short story about imprisonment with torture, cut short by a brilliantly unexpected end: Poe's 'The Pit and the Pendulum.' But now survivors of both German and Russian prison camps have begun to put their sufferings into books which, although true, are far worse than any fantasy.

The most thorough factual description of the German camps which I know is *The Theory and Practice of Hell,* by Eugen Kogon. Kogon was a South German Catholic, whom the Nazis hated for being an internationalist. His chief ideal seems to have been to help to make Europe a group of partners, instead of a crowd of hostile gangster-societies. He was arrested in 1938 when the Germans invaded Austria, and managed to survive nearly seven years in Buchenwald. His book is not a propaganda document, still less a personal statement: it is a factual report in twenty-four chapters on the social structure of the concentration camps. They formed a state within a state: a state with no citizens except the SS guards, surrounded by their slaves, their victims, and their toadies. Its population was about one million at any given time—far smaller than the present population of the Russian camps—and Kogon estimates that some eight to ten million people altogether passed through it.

The concentration-camp state was organized with a curious blend of efficiency and stupidity, which seems to have sprung from a deep conflict inside the minds of the SS themselves. Its purposes were to get a great deal of work (and hence wealth) out of the millions whom the SS considered enemies of Germany; but also to satisfy the feelings of fear, hate, and humiliation which certain sections of the German nation had developed, largely as a result of Hitler's indoctrination. So the SS worked the prisoners hard, but fed them little, put them to profitable tasks and then brutalized them into uselessness. I remember when I went to the Belsen trial, it struck me that the SS guards in the dock there were a peculiar mixture of ruthless intelligence and highly emotionalized stupidity; and sometimes, in reading Kogon's book, it is hard to resist the impression that all the guards and most of the prisoners were virtually madmen, locked up together in a huge asylum. Even when you read the terrible chapter dealing with the infamous experiments performed on living patients by the Nazi doctors (and described in conferences before such men as the Chief of the Berlin University Surgical Clinic and the Head of the German Army Medical Services) you feel that, whether the doctors knew it or not, they were just as eager to inflict pain as to make scientific discoveries.

In such a place, the chief hope of the individual prisoner was, while he could stay alive, to keep *sane*. Several books describe how this was done. There is a good short one by a British prisoner, Captain Christopher Burney, called *The Dungeon Democracy*, and a much longer and fuller one by the Norwegian philanthropist, Odd Nansen, called *Day After Day*. They both agree that it is necessary, in such conditions, to keep one's standards alive: to regard one's tormentors with hatred and contempt; to pity the Moslems who have given way, but not to imitate them; to find friends who are still sane; to maintain one's own inner life, by such small things as shaving regularly, by such complex activities as maintaining regular secret communication with the outer world. Nansen actually kept a diary 'day after day,' writing it on toilet paper, hiding it inside his bread board, smuggling it out in instalments, even illustrating it.

A recent novel deals with the same problem. This is *Spark of Life,* by Erich Maria Remarque. I think it is extremely good, though it is almost unbearably sad. It got an incomprehensible review from Anthony West in *The New Yorker*. He said it was too full of sweetness and light, and compared it detrimentally to a novel by a French survivor of the camps. And it was cruelly attacked in the *London Times Literary Supplement,* which described it roughly as a collection of artificial stories about some imaginary concentration camp: as though all fiction were not both artificial and imaginary. This seems to me quite unjust. Courage and self-sacrifice such as Remarque describes were necessary for all survivors; and I cannot see that he made the lot of his pathetic prisoners too easy. Most of them died; the survivors were ruined for life, although they retained the energy to live, if not to hope for complete recovery. And the book is full of unforgettable incidents, fundamentally true, which sum up and symbolize all the masses and millions of outrages which were documented in the trials at Nuremberg and Belsen and Buchenwald and elsewhere: the prisoner trading a dead comrade's gold tooth for a still edible dead dog; the thrush which alights on the electrified wire, and dies in an instant; the captive who never speaks, but only barks, because he went mad when police dogs were set on him; and the SS officer who believes the Americans will regard him as a soldier and rehearses his formal surrender in front of the wardrobe mirror . . .

The German camps have gone. The Russian camps remain. As far as I know, no one has yet produced a novel about them in this country. A vivid description of a Polish poet's years in Russian and Siberian prisons, given with that melancholy and ironic humor which makes the Poles one of the most intelligent and best-adjusted of nations, is *A Reluctant Traveller in Russia,* by Tadeusz Wittlin. And in 1947 there appeared a far more serious and far fuller account, with factual narratives of individual prisons. This is *The Dark Side of the Moon,* with a preface by T. S. Eliot. Thousands and thousands of families from Poland, who had committed no crime whatever except being Polish, were transported in freezing trains to camps and penal colonies in Siberia and the remote Arctic north, to work and starve and die. They are still there, working, and starving, and dying.

It is a painful subject, this. And yet sometimes the worst in man helps to produce the best. There is a continuous line of gold between Boethius writing in his condemned cell with the barbarian executioners outside, and the Polish women crammed together in a filthy airless room, singing Christmas carols to lift up their hearts.

Boethius, *The Consolation of Philosophy* (tr. J. Walton, Oxford, 1927).

P. Brickhill, *Escape or Die* (Norton, 1952).

P. Brickhill, *The Great Escape* (Norton, 1950).

C. Burney, *The Dungeon Democracy* (Heinemann, London, 1945).

C. Burney, *Solitary Confinement* (Coward-McCann, 1953).

The Dark Side of the Moon (with an introduction by T. S. Eliot, Scribner, 1947).

B. Davenport (ed.), *Great Escapes* (Sloane, 1952).

E. H. Jones, *The Road to En-Dor* (Lane, London, 1919).

A. Koestler, *Darkness at Noon* (tr. D. Hardy, Macmillan, 1941).

E. Kogon, *The Theory and Practice of Hell* (tr. H. Norden, Farrar, Straus, n.d.).

O. Nansen, *Day After Day* (tr. K. John, Putnam, 1949).

S. Péllico, *My Prisons* (tr. T. Roscoe, National Alumni, New York, 1907).

E. M. Remarque, *Spark of Life* (tr. J. Stern, Appleton-Century-Crofts, 1952).

E. E. Williams, *The Wooden Horse* (Harper, 1950).

T. Wittlin, *A Reluctant Traveller in Russia* (tr. N. E. P. Clark, Rinehart, 1952).

Index

Date Due